YOUR recipe could appear in our next cookbook!

Share your tried & true family favorites with us instantly at

www.gooseberrypatch.com

If you'd rather jot 'em down by hand, just mail this form to...
Gooseberry Patch • Cookbooks – Call for Recipes
PO Box 812 • Columbus, OH 43216-0812

If your recipe is selected for a book, you'll receive a FREE copy!

Please share only your original recipes or those that you have made your own over the years.

Recipe Name:

Number of Servings:

Any fond memories about this recipe? Special touches you like to add or handy shortcuts?

Ingredients (include specific measurements):

Instructions (continue on back if needed):

T0346097

Special Code: **cookbookspage**

Over ➤

Extra space for recipe if needed:

Tell us about yourself...

Your complete contact information is needed so that we can send you your FREE cookbook, if your recipe is published. Phone numbers and email addresses are kept private and will only be used if we have questions about your recipe.

Name:
Address:
City: State: Zip:
Email:
Daytime Phone:

Thank you! Vickie & Jo Ann

Gooseberry patch

Weeknight Dinners

☑ Monday
☑ Tuesday
☑ Wednesday
☑ Thursday
☑ Friday

Gooseberry Patch

An imprint of Globe Pequot
246 Goose Lane
Guilford, CT 06437

www.gooseberrypatch.com

1•800•854•6673

Copyright 2021, Gooseberry Patch 978-1-62093-448-7

Do you have a tried & true recipe...

tip, craft or memory that you'd like to see featured in
a **Gooseberry Patch** cookbook? Visit our website at
www.gooseberrypatch.com and follow the
easy steps to submit your favorite family recipe.
Or send them to us at:

Gooseberry Patch
PO Box 812
Columbus, OH 43216-0812

Don't forget to include the number of servings your recipe
makes, plus your name, address, phone number and email
address. If we select your recipe, your name will appear right
along with it...and you'll receive a **FREE** copy of the book!

Contents

Dedication

To every busy mom
who's ever wanted a new
answer to the question,
"What's for dinner?"

Appreciation

Thanks to all of you
who shared tried & true
recipes for satisfying
family meals...delicious
on any night of the week!

Meatless Monday

French Onion Tart

Robbi Courtaway
Webster Groves, MO

This is one of my favorite easy main dishes. It's scrumptious and very inexpensive to make. Sweet onions are delicious, but you can use any kind. I've heard that in France street vendors sell these tarts by the slice at room temperature...it's true that leftover slices are amazingly good served cold!

4 to 5 onions, thinly sliced and
    separated into rings
1-1/2 T. oil, divided

salt and pepper to taste
6-1/2 oz. pkg. pizza crust mix
1 c. shredded Swiss cheese

In a skillet over medium-high heat, sauté onions in one tablespoon oil for about 20 minutes, until light golden and caramelized. Add salt and pepper to taste. Meanwhile, prepare pizza crust mix and let stand several minutes, according to package instructions. Spread out dough in a lightly greased 12" round pizza pan; lightly coat with remaining oil. Spread onions evenly over dough. Sprinkle cheese evenly over onions. Bake on the bottom rack of oven at 425 degrees for 12 to 15 minutes, until edges of crust are golden and cheese is melted and bubbly. Cool slightly; cut into wedges. Serves 3 to 4.

A flexible plastic cutting mat makes speedy work of slicing & dicing...after chopping, just fold it in half and pour ingredients into the mixing bowl.

6

Butter Bean Soup

Krista Marshall
Fort Wayne, IN

I've been making this satisfying soup for years. We love butter beans and it's nice to have a different way to enjoy them! This recipe is also a great way to use up any leftover veggies that are tucked in the fridge.

3 T. oil
1-1/2 c. celery, chopped
1 c. carrot, peeled and chopped
1/4 c. onion, chopped
1 zucchini, chopped
salt and pepper to taste
3 T. all-purpose flour

32-oz. container vegetable or
    chicken broth
1-1/2 c. water
2 16-oz. cans baby butter
    beans, drained
1 t. dried basil

In a large soup pot, heat oil over medium heat. Add celery, carrot, onion and zucchini; season with salt and pepper. Cook, stirring often, until vegetables are soft, about 5 to 7 minutes. Sprinkle flour over vegetables; cook and stir for one minute. Gradually add broth and water; stir until smooth. Add beans, basil and additional salt and pepper, if desired. Bring to a boil. Reduce heat to low; simmer for 20 to 25 minutes, until slightly thickened. Makes 6 servings.

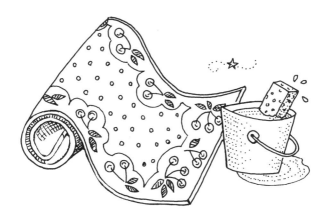

Brightly colored vintage-style oilcloth makes the best-ever tablecloth...it wipes clean in a jiffy!

Rotelle & Mushroom Skillet

Karen Sampson
Waymart, PA

This is an easy dish made in one pan...you don't even need to precook the pasta! I like to serve it with other meatless sides for a great weeknight veggie meal. My husband loves it!

2 T. butter
3 c. sliced mushrooms
1/2 c. onion, chopped
1 clove garlic, minced
4 c. water
3 cubes vegetable or chicken
    bouillon, or to taste

8-oz. pkg. rotelle pasta,
    uncooked
2/3 c. sun-dried tomatoes,
    chopped
1/3 c. grated Parmesan cheese
1/4 c. fresh parsley, chopped

Melt butter in a large skillet over medium heat. Cook mushrooms, onion and garlic until tender, about 3 minutes, stirring occasionally. Stir in water and bouillon cubes; heat to boiling. Stir in uncooked pasta and tomatoes. Reduce heat to medium; cover. Simmer for 12 minutes, stirring occasionally, or until pasta is tender and liquid is absorbed. Stir in cheese and parsley. Serves 5.

With a regular theme for each weeknight, dinner planning is a snap. Family members will look forward to each night's meal...and you'll always know the answer to "What's for dinner?"

8

Zucchini Provencal

Brenda Saylor
Tiffin, OH

This dish is a real family favorite...I usually have to double it!
Guests enjoy it too and request the recipe.

8-oz. pkg. fettuccine pasta,
    uncooked and divided
3 T. olive oil
1/2 c. onion, chopped
1 clove garlic, minced
4 c. zucchini, thinly sliced
2 to 3 tomatoes, chopped
8-oz. pkg. mozzarella cheese,
    cubed

1/2 t. dried oregano
1 t. salt
pepper to taste
Optional: 1/4 c. sliced black
    olives
Garnish: grated Parmesan
    cheese

Divide pasta in half, reserving half for use in another recipe. Cook remaining pasta according to package directions; drain. Meanwhile, heat oil in a large skillet over medium heat. Add onion and garlic; cook, stirring often, for 5 minutes. Add zucchini and tomatoes. Cook and stir for 5 minutes, or until zucchini is crisp-tender. Stir in mozzarella cheese, cooked pasta, seasonings and olives, if using. Cook, stirring gently, until heated through and mozzarella starts to melt. Serve immediately, topped with Parmesan cheese. Makes 6 servings.

Freshly grated Parmesan cheese adds extra flavor to pasta and veggie dishes. To keep a chunk of Parmesan cheese fresh longer, wrap it in a paper towel that has been moistened with cider vinegar, tuck into a plastic zipping bag and refrigerate.

Portabella-Basil Alfredo

Virginia Houser
Norristown, PA

When I serve this vegetarian recipe to my family, they don't even miss the meat! It's a great meal to make ahead and take to someone who's under the weather.

16-oz. pkg. spinach fettuccine
  pasta, uncooked
1 T. olive oil
5 portabella mushrooms,
  chopped
3 c. milk

1-1/2 t. garlic salt
8-oz. pkg. cream cheese, cubed
3-oz. pkg. cream cheese, cubed
1-1/2 t. dried basil
1-1/2 c. grated Parmesan cheese

Cook pasta according to package directions; drain. Meanwhile, heat oil in a large skillet over medium heat. Sauté mushrooms until tender, about 5 minutes; drain any extra liquid from pan. Add milk and garlic salt to skillet; heat just to boiling. Stir in both packages of cream cheese and basil. Reduce heat to low; cook, stirring constantly, until cream cheese is melted. Stir in Parmesan cheese; cook over low heat until melted, about 3 minutes. Serve over pasta. Makes 8 to 10 servings.

Steam vegetables to keep their fresh-picked taste...it's simple. Bring 1/2 inch of water to a boil in a saucepan and add cut-up veggies. Cover and cook to desired tenderness, about 3 to 5 minutes. A quick toss with a little butter or olive oil and they're ready to enjoy.

Athens Marries Rome

Kelley Nicholson
Gooseberry Patch

This tasty dish is quick to toss together for supper...it's low-fat too.
Feel free to be creative, adding or subtracting ingredients.
Your family will love it!

8-oz. pkg. penne pasta,
　uncooked
1 c. sliced mushrooms
3/4 c. canned diced tomatoes,
　drained

5 T. olive oil
10-oz. pkg. fresh spinach
3 T. balsamic vinegar, or more
　to taste
8-oz. pkg. crumbled feta cheese

Cook pasta according to package directions; drain. Meanwhile, in a
skillet over medium-high heat, sauté mushrooms and tomatoes in olive
oil until mushrooms are tender. Lower heat to medium; add spinach
and balsamic vinegar. Cook, stirring often, for a few minutes until
spinach cooks down. Mix in feta cheese and pasta. Serves 4.

Garlic Yeast Rolls

Lea Ann Burwell
Charles Town, WV

The house smells so good when I'm baking these rolls!
My kids can't get enough of them.

1/2 c. butter, melted
1 T. fresh parsley, minced
1/2 t. garlic powder

1/4 t. garlic salt
16 frozen dinner rolls, thawed

In a shallow dish, mix melted butter and seasonings. Roll each dinner
roll in butter mixture and place in a greased 8"x8" baking pan. Drizzle
any remaining butter mixture over rolls. Cover rolls and let rise until
double in size, about one hour. Bake at 350 degrees for 20 to
25 minutes, until golden. Makes 16 servings.

Zesty Black Bean Loaf

Autumn Kozak
Lake City, MI

I came up with this wonderful recipe in an effort to get my children to eat more vegetables. It's fun and my whole family likes it...even my dad, who loves his red meat!

2 16-oz. cans black beans,
  drained and rinsed
1 egg
1/2 c. catsup
1 T. Worcestershire sauce
1/2 red onion, chopped
1/2 red pepper, chopped
1/2 orange pepper, chopped

1 c. dry bread crumbs
1-1/4 oz. pkg. taco seasoning
  mix
1 to 2 t. olive oil
1 c. shredded Cheddar or
  Monterey Jack cheese
Garnish: salsa, sour cream

Combine beans, egg, catsup and Worcestershire sauce in a bowl. Beat with an electric mixer on low speed until smooth. Stir in onion, peppers, bread crumbs and seasoning mix. Brush olive oil over a 9"x5" loaf pan; transfer bean mixture to pan. Bake, uncovered, at 375 degrees for 45 minutes. Remove from oven and top with cheese; bake 10 to 15 more minutes, until cheese melts. Slice loaf; serve with salsa and sour cream. Serves 6.

From asparagus to zucchini, vegetables come in all shapes and colors! Kids can make fun placemats by clipping colorful pictures of veggies from gardening catalogs and seed packets. Arrange pictures on sheets of construction paper, then top with self-adhesive clear plastic.

Mom's Macaroni & Cheese

Billie Schettino
Kansas City, KS

Mom made this recipe for meatless Fridays. I always looked forward to it, even though I didn't like the spinach she served with it. Before I could eat my mac & cheese I had to eat at least one spoonful of spinach, which I did, and quickly washed it down with a big gulp of milk. It was worth it!

1 c. elbow macaroni, uncooked
onion powder and seasoned salt
   to taste
2 c. shredded American-Cheddar
   Jack cheese blend, divided

1 egg
1/2 c. skim milk
1/2 c. cottage cheese
2 to 3 T. butter, diced
Optional: sliced cherry tomatoes

Cook macaroni according to package directions; drain. Place half of macaroni into a 2-quart casserole dish coated with butter-flavored non-stick vegetable spray. Sprinkle macaroni with onion powder, seasoned salt and one cup shredded cheese. Repeat layering. In a food processor, process egg, milk and cottage cheese until smooth. Pour mixture over top; dot with butter. Bake, uncovered, at 350 degrees for 30 to 45 minutes, until heated through and set. Cool slightly before serving. Garnish with cherry tomatoes, if desired. Serves 2 to 4.

Give whole-grain pasta a try...it tastes great and contains more fiber than regular pasta. Check the label to be sure it's made with whole-wheat flour, not simply wheat flour.

Veggie-Stuffed Peppers

JoAnn
Gooseberry Patch

A satisfying veggie alternative to ground beef-stuffed peppers.
Sometimes I'll use red or yellow sweet peppers...their flavor is
milder than green peppers, so my kids like them best.

1 c. vegetable or chicken broth
1 c. sliced mushrooms
2/3 c. quick-cooking barley,
   uncooked
2 green peppers, halved
   lengthwise
3/4 c. shredded mozzarella
   cheese, divided

1 egg, beaten
3/4 c. tomato, chopped
1/2 c. zucchini, shredded
1/3 c. soft bread crumbs
1/2 t. dried basil
1/8 t. dried rosemary
1/8 t. onion salt
hot pepper sauce to taste

In a saucepan over medium-high heat, combine broth, mushrooms and barley. Bring to a boil; reduce heat to low. Cover and simmer for 12 to 15 minutes, until barley is tender. Drain well. Meanwhile, fill a separate saucepan with water and bring to a boil. Add pepper halves and boil for 3 minutes; drain on paper towels. In a bowl, stir together barley mixture, 1/2 cup cheese and remaining ingredients. Arrange pepper halves in an ungreased 2-quart casserole dish; fill with barley mixture. Cover and bake at 350 degrees for 20 to 25 minutes, until tender and heated through. Sprinkle remaining cheese over peppers. Return to oven until cheese melts, about 2 minutes. Makes 4 servings.

Let the kids help with meals...
a sure way to get them
interested in healthy
choices! Younger children
can scrub vegetables and tear
salad greens. Older kids can
measure, chop, stir and take
part in meal planning and shopping.
Give 'em a chance...they may just surprise you!

Chili Baked Potatoes

Melissa Olson
Brooklyn, NY

As a nutritionist, I love to share healthy recipes with my clients who love comfort food too. I serve the potatoes with steamed broccoli on the side...it's the ultimate high-fiber, low-calorie meal!

2 russet potatoes
15-oz. can vegetarian chili
1/2 c. shredded Cheddar cheese
1/2 c. salsa

2 green onions, diced
1/2 c. sliced black olives
1 tomato, diced

Pierce potatoes all over with a fork. Microwave potatoes on high setting for 9 to 12 minutes, until soft when pressed with a finger. Meanwhile, heat chili in a saucepan over medium-low heat, stirring occasionally until hot and bubbly. Slice potatoes lengthwise; top with chili and remaining ingredients. Serves 2.

Home fries, soups, casseroles...there are so many satisfying ways to fix potatoes! Whenever you bake potatoes, toss in a few extras. You'll have a head start on your next potato dish.

Slow-Cooked Minestrone

Vicky Stankus
Newton, IL

My family enjoys a meat-free meal once or twice a week. Making this soup in the slow cooker keeps the house smelling good for hours as it simmers. It's terrific with garlic bread.

4 c. vegetable or chicken broth
28-oz. can diced tomatoes
3 8-oz. cans tomato sauce
3 c. water
2 c. carrots, peeled and sliced
2 c. celery, sliced
3 cloves garlic, minced

1 T. dried, minced onion
1 T. dried basil
1 t. sea salt
1/2 t. dried oregano
1-1/2 c. multi-grain rotini pasta, uncooked

In a large slow cooker, mix together all ingredients except pasta. Cover and cook on low setting for 7 to 8 hours. About 30 minutes before serving, stir in uncooked pasta. Turn slow cooker to high setting. Cover and cook an additional 30 minutes, or until pasta is tender. Makes 8 servings.

Top bowls of soup with crunchy cheese toasts. Brush thin slices of French bread lightly with olive oil. Place on a broiler pan and broil for 2 to 3 minutes, until golden. Turn over and sprinkle with freshly grated Parmesan cheese and Italian seasoning. Broil another 2 to 3 minutes, until cheese melts. Yum!

Curried Vegetable Soup

Lynda McCormick
Burkburnett, TX

A delicious meatless meal in the slow cooker! Serve naan, an Indian-style flatbread, or crusty French bread alongside this flavorful soup.

5 to 6 c. eggplant, peeled and cut
    into 1/2-inch cubes
3 c. redskin potatoes, cut into
    1-inch cubes
15-oz. can garbanzo beans,
    drained and rinsed
14-1/2 oz. can diced tomatoes
1 T. fresh ginger, peeled and
    grated

5-1/2 t. mustard seed
5-1/2 t. coriander
1 t. curry powder
1/4 t. pepper
4 c. vegetable or chicken broth
Garnish: 2 T. fresh cilantro,
    snipped

In a large slow cooker, combine eggplant, potatoes, beans, tomatoes with juice and ginger. Sprinkle seasonings over vegetables; pour broth over all. Cover and cook on low setting for 8 to 10 hours, or on high setting for 4 to 5 hours. To serve, ladle into bowls and sprinkle with cilantro. Makes 8 to 10 servings.

Make your own flavorful vegetable broth. Coarsely chop three celery stalks with leaves, two or three large carrots, a large onion and several cloves of garlic. It's not necessary to peel the veggies. Place them in a soup pot and cover with water. Bring to a boil, then reduce heat. Simmer gently for an hour; strain. Broth may be used right away or frozen to use later.

Hearty Spinach Soup

Deborah Byrne
Clinton, CT

I love this "souper" healthy soup...it makes you feel good about eating it!

1 T. olive oil
1 onion, finely chopped
2 cloves garlic, minced
8-oz. pkg. shiitake mushrooms, thinly sliced and stems removed
6 c. low-sodium vegetable or chicken broth

1/2 t. dried rosemary
15-oz. can garbanzo beans, drained and rinsed
2 c. cooked brown rice
2 5-oz. pkgs. baby spinach
coarse salt and pepper to taste
Garnish: 1/2 c. shredded Parmesan cheese

In a Dutch oven, heat oil over medium heat. Cook onion for about 5 minutes, until tender, stirring often. Add garlic and mushrooms; cook, stirring occasionally, for about 5 minutes, until tender. Add broth and rosemary; bring to a boil. Cover and remove from heat. Add beans and cooked rice to broth mixture; return to a boil. Reduce to a simmer; cover and continue cooking for 5 minutes, to allow flavors to blend. Stir in spinach; cook just until wilted, about one minute. Season with salt and pepper. Garnish with cheese; serve immediately. Serves 6 to 8.

For thick, creamy vegetable or bean soup with no cream added, use a hand-held immersion blender to purée some of the cooked veggies right in the saucepan.

Meatless Monday

Mushroom-Barley Soup

Lisa Ashton
Aston, PA

My mom gave me this recipe...my kids really love it!

2 10-oz. pkgs. sliced
  mushrooms
1/2 c. onion, chopped
2 stalks celery, chopped
3 carrots, peeled and shredded
3 T. butter

2 14-oz. cans vegetable or
  beef broth
3-1/2 c. water
salt and pepper to taste
1/2 c. quick-cooking barley,
  uncooked

In a large saucepan over medium heat, sauté vegetables in butter, for about 5 minutes. Add broth, water, salt and pepper; bring to a boil. Reduce heat to low; simmer for about 50 minutes. Stir in barley. Cook, stirring occasionally, until barley is tender, about 10 to 12 minutes. Serves 6.

Cheddar-Dill Bread

Julie Ann Perkins
Anderson, IN

Total comfort after a busy day at work. Never miss a chance to enjoy a slice of warm bread with a mug of your favorite chili!

2 c. self-rising flour
1 T. sugar
1/4 c. butter
1 c. shredded Cheddar cheese

2 t. dill weed
1 egg
3/4 c. milk

In a large bowl, combine flour and sugar. Cut in butter with 2 knives until crumbly; stir in cheese and dill. In a small bowl, beat egg and milk; add to flour mixture and stir just until moistened. Batter will be thick. Spoon into a greased 9"x5" loaf pan. Bake at 350 degrees for 35 to 40 minutes, until bread tests done with a toothpick inserted in the center. Cool loaf in pan 10 minutes; turn out of pan and serve warm. Makes one loaf.

Get rid of an onion smell on your hands...simply hold your hands under cold running water while rubbing them with a stainless steel spoon.

Japanese Onion Soup

Staci Prickett
Montezuma, GA

This simple soup is a delicious start to a meal and also makes a very flavorful broth for cooking. I double the recipe and freeze half in ice cube trays to use later in other dishes.

8 c. water
6 cubes vegetable bouillon, or
   5 cubes beef and 1 cube
   chicken bouillon
1 celery stalk, chopped
1 carrot, peeled and chopped

1 onion, chopped
1/2 t. garlic, minced
1 c. shiitake or portabella
   mushrooms, thinly sliced
   and divided
2 green onions, sliced

In a stockpot over high heat, combine water, bouillon, celery, carrot, onion, garlic and 1/2 cup mushrooms. Bring to a boil. Cover; reduce heat to medium and simmer for 45 minutes. Strain broth, discarding vegetables. Garnish broth with remaining mushrooms and green onions. Makes 8 servings.

Add extra texture to fresh veggies of all kinds...use a crinkle cutter or a spiral slicer to cut them into slices and sticks.

Stir-Fry Veggies & Rotini

Judi Towner
Clarks Summit, PA

I created this recipe for a quick supper after a long workday, and my husband and children have always loved it. My daughter Kim liked to help chop the veggies, and it made for a great "girl chat" time. Now that she's grown, she fixes it for her own three boys. It's a super way to get them to eat their vegetables...they gobble it up!

16-oz. pkg. rotini pasta,
   uncooked
5 to 6 cloves garlic, chopped
3/4 c. butter
1-1/2 c. broccoli, cut into bite-
   size flowerets
2 c. carrots, peeled and cut into
   thin strips

1 onion, sliced
1 green or red pepper, cut into
   thin strips
Garnish: grated Parmesan
   cheese

Cook pasta according to package directions, until just tender; drain. Meanwhile, in a wok or a large, deep skillet over medium-high heat, stir-fry garlic in butter until soft and golden. Discard garlic pieces. To the remaining garlic-flavored butter, add all the vegetables. Cook and stir until crisp-tender. Add pasta and stir well. Sprinkle generously with Parmesan cheese; serve immediately. Makes 4 to 6 servings.

Stir-frying is a terrific way to make a quick and tasty dinner.
Slice veggies into equal-size pieces before you start
cooking...they'll all be done to perfection at the same time.

Homemade Fresh Basil Pesto

Pamela Stump
Chino Hills, CA

My daughter and I experimented with making our own pesto...we think we've come up with just the right ingredients and consistency!

3/4 c. pine nuts or chopped
    toasted walnuts
3 c. fresh basil, loosely packed
1 c. grated Parmesan cheese
4 cloves garlic, peeled

salt and pepper to taste
1/2 to 3/4 c. olive oil
cooked angel hair pasta, or
    sliced French bread and
    diced tomatoes

In a food processor, combine nuts, basil, cheese, garlic, salt and pepper. Process until mixed to a coarse texture. Add olive oil slowly, processing constantly at high speed to desired consistency. Add pesto to hot pasta and toss to mix. Or, for a tasty bruschetta, spread pesto on slices of toasted bread and top with diced tomatoes. Serves 4.

Tortino di Carciofi

Denise Piccirilli
Huber Heights, OH

This simple recipe for a baked artichoke omelet is a traditional Italian dish. We enjoy it very much.

2 T. olive oil
1 c. canned artichoke quarters,
    drained

4 eggs, beaten
1/2 t. salt

Heat olive oil in a skillet over medium heat. Cook artichokes, stirring frequently, for 8 to 10 minutes, until golden. Spread artichokes in a buttered one-quart casserole dish. Whisk together eggs and salt until frothy; pour over artichokes. Bake, uncovered, at 400 degrees for 15 minutes, or until firm. Cut into wedges; serve immediately. Serves 4.

Good food is the foundation of genuine happiness.

– Georges-August Escoffier

Deep-Dish Zucchini Pie

Barbara Bargdill
Gooseberry Patch

This easy, cheesy recipe is lovely for brunch or a light dinner.

9-inch deep-dish pie crust
4 c. water
4 c. zucchini, diced
4 eggs
1/2 c. onion, finely diced
1/2 c. skim milk

1/2 t. salt
1/2 t. pepper
1 c. shredded Cheddar cheese,
    divided
1/4 c. grated Parmesan cheese

Place pie crust in a 9" deep-dish pie plate; set aside. Bring water to a boil in a large saucepan; add zucchini. Reduce heat; cover and simmer until tender, about 4 minutes. Drain zucchini well in a colander, pressing with a paper towel to remove any excess liquid. In a bowl, whisk eggs until frothy. Stir in zucchini, onion, milk, salt, pepper and 2/3 cup Cheddar cheese. Pour zucchini mixture into pie crust; sprinkle with remaining Cheddar cheese and Parmesan cheese. Bake at 350 degrees for 45 minutes, or until golden and center is set. If crust edges are browning too fast, cover edges with aluminum foil. Let stand several minutes; cut into wedges. Makes 6 servings.

When chopping onions, celery or green peppers, it takes only a moment to chop some extras. Tuck them away in the freezer for a quick start to dinner another day.

Aloo Gobi Mattar

Whitney Price
British Columbia, Canada

This dish of curried potatoes and cauliflower is an easy introduction to Indian cooking...delicious and healthy! Sautéing the spices before cooking makes all the difference in flavor. East Indian and Asian markets usually stock garam masala.

3 T. oil
1-1/2 t. turmeric
3/4 t. ground cumin or cumin
   seed
3/4 t. garam masala
1/2 t. chili powder, or more
   to taste
1/2 lb. redskin potatoes, peeled
   and diced

1/2 lb. cauliflower, cut into
   bite-size flowerets
1/2 lb. fresh or frozen peas
salt to taste
2 T. fresh cilantro, chopped
   and divided

Heat oil in a large skillet over medium-high heat; add spices. Sauté for 30 seconds to one minute, just until fragrant. Add vegetables, salt and one tablespoon cilantro; stir-fry for one minute. Pour in enough water to just cover the bottom of the skillet. Reduce heat to low. Cover and cook for 10 to 15 minutes, until vegetables are fork-tender, stirring occasionally and partially mashing the vegetables. Sprinkle with remaining cilantro before serving. Makes 8 servings.

Lightly cook or blanch veggies to keep them brightly colored. Simply drop the trimmed veggies into a pan of boiling water and cook briefly until tender. Quickly immerse in ice water and drain.

Eggplant & Tomato Bake

Lanita Anderson
Chesapeake, VA

My husband and I both love tomatoes and eggplant. When I discovered this recipe several years ago, I had to try it! I tweaked it until it suited our family perfectly. It's so delicious, there are rarely any leftovers.

4 Japanese eggplants, thinly
   sliced
salt to taste
2 tomatoes, sliced
1 sweet onion, thinly sliced
1/2 t. dried basil

1/2 t. dried oregano
5 T. butter, melted and divided
1 c. shredded mozzarella cheese
1/2 c. Italian-flavored dry bread
   crumbs

Place eggplant slices in a colander in the sink. Sprinkle with salt and toss gently. Let stand for 20 to 30 minutes; rinse and drain well. Layer eggplant, tomato and onion slices in a lightly greased 13"x9" baking pan. Sprinkle with herbs; drizzle with 4 tablespoons melted butter. Cover and bake at 450 degrees for 20 minutes. Remove from oven; sprinkle with mozzarella cheese. Toss bread crumbs with remaining butter; sprinkle over cheese. Bake, uncovered, at 450 degrees for 10 minutes, or until cheese is melted and bubbly. Makes 6 to 8 servings.

Turn toss-away food jars into custom canisters...clever pantry storage for dry pasta and beans. Arrange vinyl stick-on letters on a clear glass jar, then brush on glass etching cream, following package directions. When the cream sets, peel off letters to see the name revealed like magic.

Spicy Butter Bean Burgers

Chad Rutan
Columbus, OH

These meatless burgers are pretty tasty...give 'em a try!

15-oz. can butter beans or lima
  beans, drained
1/2 c. onion, chopped
1 T. jalapeño pepper, finely
  chopped and seeds removed
6 to 8 saltine crackers, crushed
1 egg, beaten

1/2 c. shredded Cheddar cheese
1/4 t. garlic powder
salt and pepper to taste
olive oil for frying
4 whole-wheat sandwich buns,
  split

Mash beans in a bowl; mix in remaining ingredients except oil and buns. Form into 4 patties. Add 1/4 inch oil to a skillet over medium-high heat. Fry patties until golden, about 5 minutes per side, turning carefully. If baking is preferred, place patties on a greased baking sheet; bake at 400 degrees for 7 to 10 minutes per side. Serve on buns. Serves 4.

Mom's Nutty Burgers

Darrell Lawry
Kissimmee, FL

*I found this in my mom's recipe box...it was clipped from
a very old magazine. It's a hit with my family!*

3 slices whole-wheat bread, torn
1 c. milk
1 egg
1 slice onion
1 carrot, peeled and diced

1 stalk celery, diced
2 c. chopped walnuts
1 t. salt
1/4 c. butter
Optional: 8 buns

In a blender, process bread for several seconds until crumbs form. Remove crumbs to a bowl. Add milk, egg, vegetables, nuts and salt to blender. Process about 30 seconds, until chopped. Add to crumbs; mix well and form into 8 patties. Heat butter in a skillet. Cook patties for 5 minutes per side, turning carefully, until golden. Serve on buns, if desired. Makes 8 servings.

Simple Greek Salad

Lisa Ann Panzino DiNunzio
Vineland, NJ

So easy to fix...you'll be enjoying it in no time at all!

1/4 c. olive oil
3 T. cider vinegar
salt and pepper to taste
5 c. romaine lettuce, chopped

1 c. cherry tomatoes, halved
1 English cucumber, sliced
1/4 c. pitted Kalamata olives
1/3 c. crumbled feta cheese

In a large bowl, whisk together olive oil, vinegar, salt and pepper. Add lettuce, vegetables and olives. Toss gently; add cheese and toss again. Serve in salad bowls. Makes 4 servings.

Mary's Herbed Tomatoes

Sandra Smith
Quartz Hill, CA

My girlfriend made this dish for us many years ago when we visited her in Ohio. It became my favorite tomato recipe ever!

6 ripe tomatoes, sliced
1/4 c. fresh chives, finely
    chopped
1 t. salt

coarse pepper to taste
2/3 c. oil
1/4 c. cider vinegar

Layer tomato slices in a serving bowl, sprinkling chives, salt and pepper between layers. In a separate small bowl, whisk oil and vinegar together. Drizzle oil mixture over tomatoes. Cover and refrigerate at least one hour before serving. Serves 4 to 6.

Gently scrub vegetables with a damp sponge sprinkled with baking soda...it works just as well as pricey cleansers.

Spinach-Stuffed Shells

Jennifer Niemi
Nova Scotia, Canada

A great recipe fit to feed a crowd! The dish can be made in advance and refrigerated before baking. Just allow an extra 15 to 20 minutes of baking time before adding the mozzarella cheese.

24 jumbo pasta shells, uncooked
1 c. onion, finely chopped
2 10-oz. pkgs. frozen chopped
   spinach, thawed and well
   drained
3 T. olive oil
8-oz. pkg. cream cheese,
   softened
1 egg, beaten
1 T. dried basil

3/4 t. garlic powder
1-1/2 t. onion powder
1/4 t. pepper
1 c. cottage cheese
2 T. plus 1 t. grated Parmesan
   cheese
2 26-oz. jars pasta sauce
8-oz. pkg. shredded mozzarella
   cheese

Cook pasta shells according to package directions; drain. Meanwhile, in a heavy skillet over medium heat, cook onion and spinach in olive oil for 10 minutes, or until onion is soft and translucent. Set aside. In a large bowl, blend together cream cheese, egg and seasonings; stir in cottage and Parmesan cheeses. Add onion mixture; mix well. Gently spoon mixture into shells. Arrange shells in a 13"x9" baking pan sprayed with non-stick vegetable spray. Spoon pasta sauce over shells, making sure all are covered. Cover with aluminum foil. Bake at 350 degrees for 30 minutes. Remove foil; sprinkle with mozzarella cheese. Bake, uncovered, an additional 7 to 10 minutes, until cheese melts. Makes 8 to 12 servings.

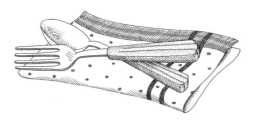

Start family meals with a gratitude circle...each person takes a moment to share two or three things that he or she is thankful for that day. It's a sure way to put everyone in a cheerful mood!

Spaghetti Squash à la Greek

Lori Drew
Ely, NV

If you're looking for a light vegetarian supper, serve this with some toasted sourdough bread and enjoy!

1 spaghetti squash, halved and
  seeds removed
1 onion, chopped
2 cloves garlic, chopped
1-1/2 T. olive oil
Optional: 1 t. basil-infused olive
  oil
1 to 2 tomatoes, chopped

4-oz. can chopped black olives,
  drained
5-oz. container crumbled feta
  cheese
2 T. balsamic vinegar
salt to taste
Garnish: chopped fresh basil

Place squash halves cut-side down on a lightly oiled baking sheet. Bake at 350 degrees for 30 minutes; cool slightly. In a skillet over medium heat, sauté onion and garlic in olive oils until tender. Transfer onion mixture to a large bowl; mix with tomatoes, olives and cheese. Pull out cooked squash strands with a fork and add to bowl. Drizzle with balsamic vinegar; add salt to taste and toss to mix. Garnish with a sprinkle of basil. Serves 4.

Soft Sesame Bread Sticks

Lynn Williams
Muncie, IN

Delicious with just about any dinner!

1-1/4 c. all-purpose flour
2 t. sugar
1-1/2 t. baking powder
1/2 t. salt

2/3 c. milk
3 T. butter, melted
2 t. sesame seed

In a small bowl, combine flour, sugar, baking powder and salt. Gradually add milk; stir to form a soft dough. Turn onto a floured surface; knead gently 3 to 4 times. Roll into a 10-inch by 5-1/2 inch rectangle; cut into 12 bread sticks. Place butter in a 13"x9" baking pan; coat bread sticks in butter and sprinkle with sesame seed. Bake at 450 degrees for 14 to 18 minutes, until golden. Makes one dozen.

Brown Butter Gnocchi

Jessica Silva
East Berlin, CT

*I love to create in the kitchen. This recipe satisfied my craving
for a hearty pasta dish with a cream sauce. Add your favorite
vegetables to the mushrooms for extra flavor!*

24-oz. pkg. frozen gnocchi,
uncooked

2 T. butter
2 portabella mushrooms, sliced

Cook gnocchi according to package directions; drain. In a large skillet
over medium heat, melt butter until browned. Add mushrooms and
gnocchi to skillet; cook until lightly golden. Add warm Parmesan
Sauce; toss to mix. Serves 2 to 4.

Parmesan Sauce:

1/3 c. all-purpose flour
3 c. milk, divided
1/4 t. nutmeg

1 c. grated Parmesan cheese
1 T. butter

Place flour in a saucepan over medium heat. Gradually add one cup
milk; whisk until smooth. Add nutmeg and remaining milk. Continue
whisking until mixture thickens and comes to a boil, about 4 minutes.
Remove from heat; stir in cheese and butter.

Just for fun, stir some quick-cooking alphabet macaroni into
a pot of vegetable soup...kids of all ages will love it!

Savory Onion-Roasted Veggies

Trysha Mapley
Alberta, Canada

A spin on potatoes roasted with onion soup mix. The carrots and pepper caramelize beautifully...the parsley and lemon liven it all up. I can't imagine roasting potatoes plain again!

1.35-oz. pkg. onion soup mix
1 lb. potatoes, quartered or
   cubed
16-oz. pkg. baby carrots
1 red pepper, cut into chunks

1/3 c. olive oil
juice of 1/2 lemon
2 T. fresh parsley, chopped
garlic powder, salt and pepper
   to taste

Combine all ingredients in a large bowl; toss to coat vegetables well. Spray a baking sheet with non-stick vegetable spray; spread mixture evenly on pan. Bake at 425 degrees, stirring every 10 minutes, for 40 minutes, or until potatoes are tender and other vegetables are golden and caramelized. Makes 4 servings.

Keep all those garden-fresh veggies fresh longer. Most veggies should be kept in the refrigerator with the exception of potatoes, sweet potatoes, onions and eggplant. Tomatoes will also keep their sun-ripened flavor best if stored on the windowsill or counter.

Cold Soba Noodle Salad

Sandra Sullivan
Aurora, CO

I've served this chilled salad at tailgates and received rave reviews!
Use whole-wheat angel hair pasta instead of soba noodles,
if you wish.

15-oz. pkg. soba noodles,
  uncooked
1-1/2 t. sesame oil
1/3 c. rice vinegar
1/3 c. soy sauce
juice and zest of 1 lime
2 T. brown sugar, packed

2 cloves garlic, minced
2 t. red pepper flakes, or more to
  taste
1 c. carrot, peeled and finely
  grated
1/4 c. peanuts, coarsely chopped
1/2 c. fresh cilantro, chopped

Break noodles into 3-inch lengths; cook according to package directions. Drain and rinse with cold water; set aside. In a large bowl, combine remaining ingredients except carrot, peanuts and cilantro; stir until sugar dissolves. Stir in noodles and remaining ingredients; cover and refrigerate at least one hour. Toss salad again just before serving; add a little more soy sauce and vinegar if mixture seems dry. Serve chilled. Makes 8 servings.

Whip up a jarful of homemade buttermilk dressing...wonderful on tossed salads and a delicious dip for fresh veggies too. Blend 1/2 cup buttermilk, 1/2 cup mayonnaise, one teaspoon dried parsley, 1/2 teaspoon onion powder, 1/4 teaspoon garlic powder, 1/8 teaspoon dill weed and a little salt and pepper. Keep refrigerated.

Sesame-Asparagus Salad

Kathy Milligan
Mira Loma, CA

*Our family loves this salad in springtime when asparagus
is fresh...it tastes terrific and is easy to prepare.*

1-1/2 lbs. asparagus, cut
    diagonally into 2-inch pieces
3 T. toasted sesame oil
1 t. white wine vinegar

4 t. soy sauce
2-1/2 T. sugar or honey
4 t. toasted sesame seed

Bring a large saucepan of water to a boil over high heat. Add
asparagus; cook for 2 to 3 minutes, just until crisp-tender. Immediately
drain asparagus; rinse with cold water until asparagus is completely
cooled. Drain again; pat dry. Cover and refrigerate until chilled, about
one hour. In a small bowl, whisk together remaining ingredients; cover
and refrigerate. At serving time, drizzle asparagus with dressing; toss
to coat. Makes 4 to 6 servings.

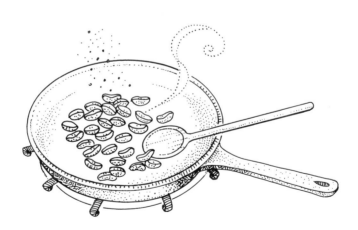

Toasting really brings out the flavor of sesame seed and chopped
nuts...and it's simple. Add seeds or nuts to a small dry skillet. Cook
and stir over low heat for a few minutes, until toasty and golden.

Lentil & Brown Rice Tacos

Jennifer Fleener
Vernon Hills, IL

Going vegetarian was an easy transition for my family. But if you're just giving meatless meals a try, I think this recipe has all the flavor and texture of tacos made with beef.

1 T. olive oil
1/2 c. onion, diced
1 to 2 cloves garlic, minced
2 t. chili powder
1/2 t. ground cumin
3/4 c. long-cooking brown rice, uncooked
3/4 c. dried brown lentils, uncooked

4 c. vegetable broth
salt and pepper to taste
6 to 8 6-inch corn or flour tortillas
Garnish: shredded lettuce, sliced avocado, diced tomatoes, sour cream, salsa, shredded Cheddar cheese

Heat olive oil in a medium saucepan over medium heat. Sauté onion for about 4 minutes. Add garlic and spices; cook for about one minute to toast spices. Add rice; stir to coat rice in spices. Add lentils and broth; bring to a boil. Reduce heat to a simmer; cover and cook for about 45 to 50 minutes, until rice and lentils are tender. Remove from heat; fluff with a fork and season with salt and pepper. Spoon mixture onto tortillas and top with your favorite taco fixings. Serves 6 to 8.

A veggie sub sandwich is a wonderful spin on the traditional meat-filled sub. Load layers of fresh or roasted veggie slices on kaiser rolls and drizzle with Italian salad dressing.

Meatless Monday

Chile Relleno Casserole

Gerri Bowers
Farwell, TX

My mom served this when I was a child, and I've always loved it.
Serve it with Spanish rice and refried beans...yum!

16-oz. pkg. shredded Monterey
  Jack cheese
16-oz. pkg. shredded Cheddar
  cheese
2 8-oz. cans whole green chiles

4 eggs, separated
1 T. all-purpose flour
2/3 c. evaporated milk
salt and pepper to taste

Sprinkle both packages of cheese into a lightly greased 13"x9" baking pan. Arrange chiles over cheese; set aside. Beat egg yolks in a bowl; gradually beat in flour and milk. In a separate bowl, beat egg whites until fluffy; stir into yolk mixture. Add salt and pepper to taste. Drizzle egg mixture over chiles. Bake, uncovered, at 325 degrees for 50 minutes. Let stand several minutes before serving. Makes 8 servings.

Crispy Corn Fritters

Karen Puchnick
Butler, PA

So easy to make...delicious with all kinds of other dishes!

1 c. biscuit baking mix
1/2 c. milk
1 egg
1 c. frozen corn, thawed

pepper to taste
2 T. oil
Garnish: honey

In a bowl, stir together baking mix, milk and egg until just blended. Stir in corn; season with pepper. Let batter stand for 5 to 10 minutes. Heat oil in a skillet over medium heat. Drop batter into oil with a large spoon. Cook until golden; turn and cook one minute on the other side. Drain on paper towels. Serve drizzled with a little honey. Makes 6 to 8 servings.

Very Veggie Lasagna

Lanita Anderson
Chesapeake, VA

You'll love cooking up all your garden bounty in this recipe. The combination of veggies makes it not only tasty, but also healthy!

9 lasagna noodles, uncooked
2 T. olive oil
1 bunch broccoli, cut into
   bite-size flowerets
2 carrots, peeled and cut into
   thin sticks
2 zucchini, thinly sliced
2 yellow squash, thinly sliced

1 onion, sliced
1/2 green pepper, thinly sliced
1/2 red pepper, thinly sliced
2 cloves garlic, minced
salt and pepper to taste
28-oz. jar pasta sauce, divided
4 c. shredded mozzarella cheese,
   divided

Cook lasagna noodles according to package directions; drain. Meanwhile, heat oil in a large skillet or wok over medium-high heat. Add vegetables, garlic, salt and pepper to skillet. Cook and stir until crisp-tender, about 10 minutes. Spread 3/4 cup pasta sauce in a greased 13"x9" baking pan. Arrange 3 lasagna noodles over sauce; layer with 1/3 each of vegetable mixture, pasta sauce and cheese. Repeat layers 2 more times, ending with cheese on top. Cover and bake at 350 degrees for 60 to 65 minutes, until hot and bubbly. Let stand for 15 minutes before cutting into squares. Makes 10 to 12 servings.

A can't-go-wrong mix of vintage and new tableware is always a fun and different way to serve up dinner...so go ahead and choose all your favorites.

Cheesy Tomatoes & Lentils

Alison Gerrits
Alberta, Canada

When my sister-in-law served this dish to us years ago, it was the first time I'd tried lentils. Now, everyone loves this quick, hearty vegetarian meal...and my kids are picky eaters! They like to stir in the mozzarella cheese and watch it melt. Warm up any leftovers for lunch.

2 T. olive oil
2 to 3 cloves garlic, pressed
1 t. chili garlic sauce
1/2 t. salt
16-oz. can lentils, drained and
  rinsed
14-1/2 oz. can diced tomatoes
1/2 t. onion powder
1/2 t. dried basil
1/2 t. dried oregano
cooked basmati rice
Garnish: shredded mozzarella
  cheese

Heat olive oil in a large wok or saucepan. Add garlic, chili garlic sauce and salt. Cook about one minute, until garlic is fragrant but not browned. Add lentils, tomatoes with juice and seasonings; stir. Cover and bring to a boil. Lower heat to medium-low; cover and simmer for 10 to 15 minutes. Serve in pasta bowls over hot cooked rice; sprinkle with cheese as desired. Serves 4.

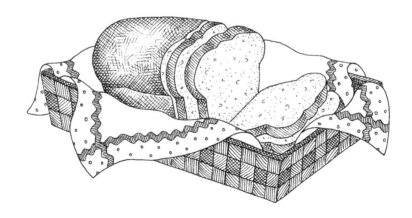

Make a scrumptious topping for veggies using leftover bread or rolls. Sauté soft bread crumbs in olive oil until crisp and golden...sprinkle with chopped herbs for extra flavor.

Cheddar Baked Spaghetti

Carol McKeon
Lebanon, TN

This is my version of a meatless dish my mother often made for us...it was our favorite Friday dinner. My brother and I still love it, as it always reminds us of Mom.

16-oz. pkg. thin spaghetti, uncooked
1/2 c. butter, softened
16-oz. jar double Cheddar cheese pasta sauce

12-oz. can tomato paste
2 T. sugar
1/3 c. Italian-flavored dry bread crumbs
Garnish: shredded

Cook spaghetti according to package directions, just until tender. Drain; return to cooking pot. Add butter; toss spaghetti until butter melts. Stir in pasta sauce, tomato paste and sugar. Transfer to a greased 13"x9" baking pan; sprinkle with bread crumbs. Bake, uncovered, at 350 degrees for 35 minutes, or until bubbly and crunchy on top. Serves 6 to 8.

Old-Fashioned Spaghetti

Eileen Gelbmann
Houston, TX

My sister and I loved this comforting dish. It was the most asked-for dish our mother made...a favorite on meatless Fridays during Lent. I like to add some freshly ground pepper for zip.

8-oz. pkg. spaghetti, uncooked
2 T. margarine
1/2 c. onion, finely minced
1/4 c. green pepper, finely minced

1 clove garlic, finely minced
10-3/4 oz. can tomato soup
3 slices American cheese, torn into small pieces
Optional: pepper to taste

Cook spaghetti according to package directions; drain. Meanwhile, melt margarine in a skillet over medium heat. Sauté onion, green pepper and garlic until tender. Add soup; cook until bubbly. Add cheese, stirring constantly until melted. To serve, ladle sauce over cooked spaghetti; toss to mix well. Sprinkle with pepper, if desired. Serves 4.

Vegetarian Meatballs

Sandy Roy
Crestwood, KY

Whenever I take these yummy meatballs to a potluck, the dish comes back empty! For convenience, the unbaked meatballs may be frozen separately, then topped with sauce when they're baked.

1 onion, finely minced
1/4 c. oil
5 eggs, beaten
1 T. soy sauce
1 t. smoke-flavored cooking sauce
1 t. celery salt
1 c. frozen textured vegetable protein crumbles, thawed

2 c. chopped pecans
1-1/2 c. Italian-flavored dry bread crumbs
1-1/2 c. finely shredded mozzarella cheese
2 to 3 cloves garlic, finely chopped

In a skillet over medium heat, sauté onion in oil until tender; cool slightly. In a bowl, whisk together eggs, sauces and celery salt; set aside. Pulse crumbles several times in a food processor to break up; add to a large bowl. Add onion, egg mixture and remaining ingredients; stir well. Form into walnut-size balls with a small cookie scoop. Arrange in a 13"x9" baking pan coated with non-stick vegetable spray. Top each with a spoonful of BBQ Sauce. Cover with aluminum foil; bake at 350 degrees for 45 minutes. Serves 10.

BBQ Sauce:

1 onion, finely minced
1/4 c. butter
1 c. catsup
1/3 c. brown sugar, packed

2 T. chili powder
1/2 t. smoke-flavored cooking sauce

Sauté onion in butter until tender. Stir in remaining ingredients and simmer for 5 minutes.

Fresh herbs give a wonderful flavor boost to vegetable dishes!
If a recipe calls for one teaspoon of a dried herb, simply substitute one tablespoon of the fresh herb.

Farmhouse Quiche

Sonya Labbe
Los Angeles, CA

This delicious quiche recipe is always a hit at brunch or dinner. Salsa and sour cream make great toppings for this veggie-packed quiche....scrumptious!

9-inch pie crust
2 T. olive oil
1/2 red pepper, diced
1/2 green pepper, diced
2 cloves garlic, minced
1/4 c. zucchini, diced
2 T. fresh basil, chopped
4 eggs, beaten

1 c. half-and-half
1 t. salt
1/2 t. pepper
8-oz. pkg. shredded Pepper
   Jack cheese
1/3 c. grated Parmesan cheese
3 plum tomatoes, sliced

Place crust in a 9" pie plate; pierce bottom and sides with a fork. Bake at 425 degrees for 10 minutes; set aside. Heat oil in a large skillet over medium heat; sauté peppers, garlic, zucchini and basil until tender. Whisk together eggs, half-and-half, salt and pepper in a large bowl. Stir in pepper mixture and cheeses. Pour into pie crust and top with sliced tomatoes. Bake at 375 degrees for 45 minutes. Let stand 5 minutes before slicing. Serves 6.

All kinds of vegetables become deliciously sweet when roasted... asparagus, carrots, squash, bell peppers and Brussels sprouts, just to name a few. Toss peeled, sliced veggies with olive oil and spread on a baking sheet. Bake at 350 degrees for about 30 minutes, stirring occasionally, until tender.

Golden Oat Muffins

Cindy Buchanan
Charlestown, IN

*There's nothing better than a basket of fresh-baked bread
at dinner...and everybody loves these muffins!*

1 c. long-cooking oats, uncooked	1/2 t. salt
1 c. milk	2 T. shortening
1 c. all-purpose flour	1/4 c. sugar
1 T. baking powder	1 egg, beaten

Process oats in a food processor or blender until ground; place in a large bowl. Add milk to oats; let stand for 5 minutes. In a separate bowl, sift together flour, baking powder and salt; set aside. In another small bowl, beat shortening with sugar until light and fluffy. Add egg; stir until smooth. Stir shortening mixture into oat mixture. Add flour mixture and stir just until mixed. Fill greased muffin cups 2/3 full. Bake at 350 degrees for 25 minutes. Makes one dozen.

House-Blend Seasoning

Hope Davenport
Portland, TX

*This is terrific for low-sodium diets. It has so much more flavor than
plain salt. A small jar of it makes a great little gift too.*

5 t. onion powder	1 t. dried thyme
1 T. garlic powder	1/2 t. celery seed
1 T. paprika	1/2 t. white pepper
1 T. dry mustard	

Mix all ingredients together and store in a shaker. Use like salt and pepper to season food during cooking and at the table. Makes about 1/3 cup.

Tuck a terra-cotta warming tile into a napkin-lined basket of freshly baked rolls or muffins to keep them warm and tasty all through dinner.

Incredible Potato-Mushroom Soup
Kara Azevedo
Rapid City, SD

One of my favorite soups! It's delicious, vegetarian-friendly and is great when you are in the mood for a flavorful broth-based soup. My guests always compliment me on it.

2 T. butter
3 cloves garlic, minced
5 shallots, diced
16-oz. pkg. cremini mushrooms, chopped
1/4 t. poultry seasoning
1/8 t. dried oregano

1/8 t. nutmeg
salt and pepper to taste
1 c. russet potato, peeled and diced
5 c. water
1 cube vegetable bouillon

Melt butter in a deep oven-proof skillet over medium-low heat. Add garlic and shallots. Cook until soft and golden, about 10 minutes. Reduce heat if they are cooking too fast. Add mushrooms and seasonings. Cook for about 10 minutes, until softened. Add potato, water and bouillon cube; bring to a boil. Reduce heat; simmer for 15 minutes. Cover skillet and bake at 350 degrees for 30 to 45 minutes. Makes 4 servings.

At farmers' markets and even at the supermarket, watch for heirloom vegetables...varieties that Grandma might have grown in her garden. These veggies don't always look picture-perfect, but their flavor can't be beat!

Black Bean Soup

Karen Marano
New Richmond, WI

*A wonderfully yummy and easy recipe that's healthy
too...you'll have no regrets about eating a second bowl!
Add any other vegetables you like.*

1 c. onion, chopped
1 to 2 T. olive oil
1 c. celery, chopped
1 c. green, red or yellow pepper, chopped
4 c. tomato juice or vegetable cocktail juice
14-oz. can fat-free vegetable or chicken broth
16-oz. can black beans, plain or with jalapeño peppers, drained
salt and pepper to taste
Garnish: sour cream, shredded Cheddar cheese, sliced green onions

In a soup pot over medium heat, sauté onion in oil until softened. Add remaining ingredients except garnish. Simmer for about 30 minutes, stirring occasionally. Add desired toppings to individual bowls of soup. Makes 4 servings.

Keep the week's menu plans at a glance. Tack extra-wide rick-rack to a bulletin board and just slip your grocery list underneath.

Old-Time Carrot Cake

Debbie Adkins
Lexington, KY

*This simple recipe was passed down from my grandmother.
I think the buttermilk glaze is much tastier than the usual
cream cheese icing, and it doesn't take long to whip together.*

2 c. all-purpose flour
1 t. baking powder
1/4 t. salt
1 t. cinnamon

1-1/4 c. oil
2 c. sugar
4 eggs
2 c. carrots, peeled and grated

In a medium bowl, sift together flour, baking powder, salt and
cinnamon; set aside. In a separate large bowl, combine oil and sugar;
mix well. Beat in eggs, one at a time, until well mixed. Stir in carrots.
Fold in flour mixture and mix well. Pour into a greased and floured
13"x9" baking pan. Bake at 350 degrees for about 40 minutes, until
a toothpick inserted in center comes out clean. Remove from oven.
Immediately use a fork to poke holes in cake and drizzle Buttermilk
Glaze over cake. Store at room temperature. This cake is actually better
after it stands for a day or two, as the glaze becomes sugary and crisp.
Makes 12 to 18 servings.

Buttermilk Glaze:

1/2 c. buttermilk
1 c. sugar

1/2 t. baking soda
1 T. light corn syrup

Combine all ingredients in a bowl; blend until well mixed.

Whip up some fruit smoothies for a healthy treat...they're especially
delectable with summer-ripe peaches, berries and bananas! In a
blender, combine 2 cups fruit with one cup vanilla yogurt,
one cup ice cubes and one tablespoon honey. Blend until
smooth; pour into tall glasses and enjoy.

Whole-Wheat Applesauce Bars *Cassandra Gleason*
Fond du Lac, WI

A very yummy cake recipe that I received from my momma.

1/3 c. butter, softened	1/2 c. all-purpose flour
2/3 c. brown sugar, packed	1/2 t. baking soda
2 eggs, beaten	2/3 c. cinnamon applesauce
3/4 t. allspice	1/3 c. chopped walnuts
1/2 c. whole-wheat flour	1/3 c. golden raisins

In a large bowl, beat together butter, brown sugar, eggs and allspice until well blended. In a separate bowl, stir together flours and baking soda. Add to butter mixture, stirring well. Add remaining ingredients; mix well. Spread batter in a greased 9"x9" baking pan. Bake at 350 degrees for 25 to 30 minutes; cool. Spread with Cream Cheese Frosting; cut into bars. Makes 9 servings.

Cream Cheese Frosting:

1/2 c. butter, softened	1 t. vanilla extract
8-oz. pkg. cream cheese, softened	1 to 2 c. powdered sugar

In a large bowl, beat together butter and cream cheese until fluffy. Stir in vanilla. Gradually add powdered sugar to desired thickness.

Use empty tin cans with bright veggie labels to hold simple bouquets of black-eyed susans, zinnias, daisies and other cut flowers. Line them up along the center of your table...charming!

Anytime Frozen Fruit Cups

Amy Butcher
Columbus, GA

I usually have a batch of these refreshing treats tucked away
in my freezer. It's a snap to pull out a few cups whenever I need
a quick snack, salad or dessert.

10-oz. jar maraschino cherries,
   drained and divided
11-oz. can mandarin oranges,
   drained and divided
8-oz. pkg. cream cheese,
   softened

1/2 c. sugar
8-oz. can crushed pineapple,
   drained
Optional: 1/2 c. chopped pecans
8-oz. container frozen whipped
   topping, thawed

Halve 9 cherries; chop remaining cherries. Reserve halved cherries
and 18 orange sections for garnish. In a large bowl, beat cream cheese
and sugar until fluffy. Add chopped cherries, pineapple and pecans, if
using. Fold in whipped topping and remaining oranges. Spoon mixture
into 18 muffin cups lined with aluminum foil cupcake liners. Garnish
each cup with a halved cherry and an orange section. Cover and freeze
until firm. Let stand at room temperature 10 minutes before serving.
Makes 1-1/2 dozen.

Cook up a simple cinnamon sauce to drizzle over fresh fruit. In a
saucepan, combine 1/2 cup sugar, 2 tablespoons cornstarch and
2 cinnamon sticks. Stir in a 5-ounce can of evaporated milk. Cook
and stir over medium heat until mixture boils and thickens.
Discard cinnamon sticks; stir in 1-1/2 teaspoons vanilla extract.
Chill for 2 hours before serving; keep refrigerated.

Tuesday is
Tex-Mex
Night

Mexicali Chicken Stack-Ups

Sue Wright
Killeen, TX

A family favorite! I took a recipe we all enjoyed and tweaked it to include even more ingredients we like...yummy!

4 10-inch flour tortillas, divided
2 boneless, skinless chicken
   breasts, cooked and diced or
   shredded
3/4 c. salsa
1/4 c. sliced black olives

1 t. ground cumin
1 c. shredded Cheddar cheese,
   divided
Garnish: sour cream, olives,
   sliced green onions

Place one tortilla in the bottom of a lightly greased 2-quart round casserole dish; set aside. In a bowl, mix chicken, salsa, olives, cumin and 3/4 cup cheese. Spoon 1/3 of chicken mixture over tortilla in dish. Repeat layering, ending with the last tortilla. Sprinkle with remaining cheese. Cover with aluminum foil. Bake at 350 degrees for 30 to 35 minutes, until hot and bubbly, uncovering for the final 5 minutes. Cut into wedges and serve with sour cream. Makes 2 to 4 servings.

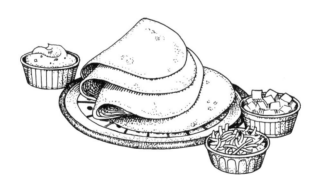

Tortillas come in several different sizes and types...you may even be able to find sopes, which are small thick corn disks with a raised edge. Here's a handy size guide:

For tacos, use 6-inch tortillas
For fajitas, use 8-inch tortillas
For burritos, use 10-inch tortillas

Tuesday is **Tex-Mex Night**

Grandpa Jackson's Burritos

Pamela Bennett
Whittier, CA

These burritos are delicious...everybody loves them! Terrific for parties, or freeze them individually for the kids to zap in the microwave. This recipe was my grandfather's when he was an Army cook during World War II. He lived with us until he passed away, about the time I entered high school. It's one of many recipes he passed down to my mom.

1 lb. ground beef
1 lb. ground pork sausage
1 lb. chorizo pork or beef link
    sausage, casings removed
2 15-1/2 oz. cans chili beans
minced garlic or garlic powder
    to taste

16-oz. pkg. shredded Cheddar
    cheese
16-oz. pkg. shredded Monterey
    Jack cheese
1 doz. 10-inch flour tortillas

In a large skillet over medium-high heat, sauté beef and pork sausage together until browned; drain and set aside in a bowl. In the same skillet, sauté chorizo sausage until browned; drain. Stir in beef mixture, beans and garlic or garlic powder. Cook over medium-low heat for 10 to 20 minutes, stirring often. Add cheeses. Cook, stirring constantly, for another 15 to 20 minutes. Mash lightly with a potato masher; let cool for 10 to 15 minutes. To serve, scoop mixture onto tortillas and roll up. Makes one dozen.

Salsa is flavorful, naturally fat-free and tasty on so many more foods than just tacos! Red or green, mild or hot, thin or chunky style...try a spoonful of salsa as a topper for grilled chicken, burgers, hot dogs and even omelets.

Fiesta Chicken Soft Tacos

Mandy Doolittle
Highlands Ranch, CO

Family & friends beg me to make these simple and scrumptious tacos. The recipe can easily be doubled to feed a hungry crowd.

2 T. oil
1/2 yellow onion, diced
1/2 green pepper, diced
2 to 3 cloves garlic, minced
1 lb. boneless, skinless chicken
  breasts, cubed

1 to 2 T. taco seasoning mix
1-1/2 c. chunky salsa
4 6-inch flour tortillas
Garnish: shredded Cheddar
  cheese or other favorite
  toppings

Heat oil in a skillet over medium heat. Add onion, green pepper and garlic; sauté until tender. Add chicken; cook until no longer pink, about 5 to 8 minutes. Stir in taco seasoning and salsa; simmer for 3 minutes. To serve, spoon mixture onto tortillas. Fold over once; garnish as desired. Makes 4 servings.

A speedy side for any south-of-the-border supper. Stir spicy salsa and shredded cheese into hot cooked rice. Cover and let stand a few minutes, until the cheese melts. Sure to please!

Tuesday is Tex-Mex Night

Southwestern Turkey Bake

Regina Wickline
Pebble Beach, CA

Real comfort food...easy to toss together on a busy weeknight!
It's a great way to use leftover roast turkey, or substitute
a rotisserie chicken from the deli.

10-3/4 oz. can cream of chicken
soup
10-3/4 oz. can cream of
mushroom soup
1 c. sour cream
7-oz. can diced green chiles,
drained

16 6-inch corn tortillas, cut into
strips and divided
1 to 1-1/2 c. cooked turkey,
shredded and divided
8-oz. pkg. shredded Cheddar
cheese, divided

In a bowl, combine soups, sour cream and chiles; set aside. Arrange
half of the tortilla strips in a lightly greased 13"x9" baking pan. Layer
with half each of the turkey, soup mixture and cheese. Repeat layers,
ending with cheese. Bake, uncovered, at 350 degrees for 30 to
35 minutes, until heated through and cheese is bubbly. Makes 6 to
8 servings.

Homemade guacamole is scrumptious, and it's oh-so easy to make.
Cut 4 ripe avocados in half, remove the pits and scoop into a bowl.
Add a chopped onion, 2 minced cloves garlic, 2 tablespoons of
lime juice and a dash of salt. Mash it up and serve with
crisp tortilla chips...it can't be beat!

Tex-Mex Chicken & Rice

Tracy Long
Bellwood, NE

I created this recipe with ingredients I had on hand. My family raved about it, and now I make it often. A slow cooker and everyday ingredients...what could be easier?

3 to 4 boneless, skinless chicken breasts
10-3/4 oz. can cream of chicken soup
10-oz. can diced tomatoes with green chiles
1 c. salsa verde
1 t. ground cumin

1 c. quick-cooking brown rice, uncooked
1-1/2 c. fresh or frozen corn
Garnish: shredded Cheddar cheese, sour cream, tortilla chips, diced avocado, sliced black olives

Place chicken in a slow cooker. In a bowl, blend soup, tomatoes with juice, salsa and cumin; spoon over chicken. Cover and cook on low setting for 4 hours, or until chicken is very tender. Shred chicken with 2 forks and return to slow cooker. Add uncooked rice and corn; stir to combine. Cover and cook on low setting for an additional 2 hours, or until rice is tender. Serve with desired garnishes. Makes 6 to 8 servings.

Shred a block of cheese in a jiffy. Freeze wrapped cheese for 10 to 20 minutes...it will just glide across the grater!

Texas Hominy

Rita Barnett
Lewisburg, TN

I got this recipe from my aunt, who lived in Texas for several years while her husband was stationed there in the Air Force. When my son's school cafeteria asked for recipes to serve to the students, this turned out to be quite popular. My teenage son has often eaten at least half of it in one sitting!

15-1/2 oz. can hominy, drained
15-oz. can chili
2 c. tortilla or corn chips, crushed

1-1/2 to 2 c. shredded Cheddar
   or Mexican-blend cheese

In a lightly greased 9"x9" baking pan, combine hominy and chili. Top with chips and cheese. Bake, uncovered, at 350 degrees for 25 to 30 minutes, until heated through and cheese melts. Serves 4.

5-Can Mexican Meal

Brenda Hughes
Houston, TX

In a hurry, I opened five cans from my pantry and made the best one-pot meal ever! Quick and hearty...triple it to feed a crowd!

15-oz. can beef tamales,
   unwrapped and cut into
   1-inch pieces
16-oz. can light red kidney
   beans

16-oz. can pinto beans
11-oz. can sweet corn and diced
   peppers
10-oz. can diced tomatoes with
   green chiles

Combine all ingredients in a large saucepan without draining cans. Cook over medium heat, stirring occasionally, until hot and bubbly. Serves 6.

Lots of Tex-Mex and Mexican recipes call for crushed tortilla chips...what a thrifty use for the broken chips left at the bottom of the bag!

Mild Chili Verde

*Alta Padilla
Riverside, CA*

*My husband and I are empty nesters now. But if I mention I'm going
to put this into my slow cooker, my kids all come home to eat. I even
made this dish for 250 guests at a 25th wedding anniversary dinner!
Serve with Mexican rice and refried beans.*

4 lbs. boneless pork country
   ribs, cut into 1-inch cubes
garlic salt to taste
2 T. oil
2 onions, chopped
2 7-oz. cans diced green chiles
14-1/2 oz. can diced tomatoes

24-oz. can thick & chunky salsa
   verde
1 c. water
2 t. chicken bouillon granules
1/2 t. ground cumin
flour tortillas, warmed

Season pork with garlic salt. Heat oil in a large skillet over medium-
high heat. Working in batches, brown pork on all sides; remove
pork to a slow cooker as it is browned. Drain skillet, reserving
one tablespoon oil in skillet. Add onions and sauté until translucent,
scraping to get up all of the browned bits in the skillet. Add onions,
undrained chiles and tomatoes to slow cooker; stir in salsa, water,
bouillon and cumin. Cover and cook on low setting for 6 to 8 hours,
or on high setting for 3 hours, until pork is very tender. To serve,
shred pork; spoon into warmed tortillas. Makes 8 to 10 servings.

All-day slow cooking is ideal for less-tender cuts of meat like
pork shoulder and beef chuck roast. They'll turn out juicy and
falling-apart tender...just right for many Mexican dishes.

Shredded Mexican Chicken

Kimberly Perry
Collierville, TN

I use this basic chicken recipe for everything! It's so easy to fix in the slow cooker. It makes a wonderful filling for tacos, enchiladas and nachos...the whole family loves it.

2-1/2 lbs. boneless, skinless
    chicken breasts and/or
    thighs
3 c. chicken broth

2 T. chili powder
1 t. dried oregano
1 t. garlic powder

Place chicken in a slow cooker. Pour in broth; sprinkle with seasonings. Cover and cook on low setting for 4 to 6 hours, until chicken is tender. Remove chicken and shred with 2 forks. Serve as desired in tacos, enchiladas or nachos. Serves 8.

Flour tortillas are tastiest when warmed. Stack tortillas between moistened paper towels and microwave on high setting for 20 to 30 seconds...easy!

Sopa de Albondigas

Katharine Stroud
Modesto, CA

This recipe for meatball soup came from my great-grandmother, then was shared with all the women in my family. I've passed it on to my children too, three boys who love to cook. It's wonderful for potlucks and cold winter days. I have added the turkey option for a reduced-calorie diet. Either way, it's perfect!

1 lb. ground beef or turkey	2 cubes beef bouillon
1/2 c. cooked white rice	2 potatoes, peeled and diced
1/2 c. onion, diced	2 carrots, peeled and diced
1 egg, beaten	2 stalks celery, diced
granulated garlic to taste	1/2 c. zucchini, diced
salt and pepper to taste	1/2 c. fresh cilantro, chopped
6 to 8 c. water	

In a large bowl, combine meat, rice, onion and egg. Season with garlic, salt and pepper. Form into one-inch meatballs; set aside. In a large soup pot over medium-high heat, bring water to a boil. Add meatballs and bouillon cubes; reduce heat and simmer for about 20 minutes. Add vegetables; simmer for about 30 more minutes, until vegetables are tender. Stir in cilantro. Season with additional garlic, salt and pepper, if desired. Serves 4 to 6.

Food is a wonderful way to learn about other places and cultures! Set the mood with background music...stop by the local library and pick up some CDs of mariachi or salsa music to enjoy at dinnertime.

Chopper's Chipotle Pork Chili

Yvette Garza
Livingston, CA

"Chopper" Scott is a friend of mine...we both love to ride motorcycles. I got this basic recipe from him and tweaked it. It's very yummy, especially with corn muffins.

3-lb. boneless pork roast
2 to 3 t. oil
2 onions, chopped
5 cloves garlic, chopped
3 tomatoes, chopped

3 16-oz. cans black-eyed peas, drained
1/2 c. canned chipotle peppers in adobo sauce
salt and pepper to taste

Place pork roast in a slow cooker; add enough water to cover roast. Cover and cook on high setting for 4 to 6 hours, until roast is very tender. Shortly before roast is done, heat oil in a large soup pot over medium heat. Sauté onion and garlic; stir in tomatoes. Shred roast with 2 forks and transfer to soup pot; stir in peas. Purée peppers with sauce in a food processor; add to soup pot. Season with salt and pepper to taste. Warm through, stirring occasionally. Makes 8 to 10 servings.

Quesadillas are really just Mexican grilled cheese! They're quick and filling paired with a bowl of soup or even as an after-school snack. Sandwich shredded or sliced cheese between two flour tortillas. Cook on both sides in a lightly greased skillet until the cheese melts. Cut into wedges and serve with salsa.

Green Chile Soup

Bernadette Torres
Monte Vista, CO

I have many fond memories of winter nights, savoring this
slow-cooker soup with fresh-baked biscuits or cornbread.

1 lb. ground beef
1/2 c. onion, chopped
1 clove garlic, chopped
5 russet potatoes, peeled and
   diced

1/2 c. chopped green chiles
1.35-oz. pkg. onion soup mix
6 to 8 c. water, divided
salt and pepper to taste

Brown beef, onion and garlic in a skillet over medium heat; drain. In a
slow cooker, combine potatoes, chiles, soup mix and 6 cups water; stir
in beef mixture. Add remaining water to cover ingredients as necessary.
Cover and cook on low setting for 5 hours. Add salt and pepper to
taste. Serves 4.

Be sure to include family members in meal planning, grocery
shopping and cooking. Picky eaters are much more likely to eat
food that they've helped to choose and prepare themselves!

Tuesday is **Tex-Mex Night**

Shredded Mexican Beef

Nancy Albers Shore
Cheyenne, WY

I adapted this slow-cooker recipe from a newspaper article, changing the seasonings to suit my family. We love it spooned over hot cooked rice with beans on the side. Serve it in tortillas, tacos or just about any way your family can think of.

2 green peppers, sliced
1 onion, sliced
2-lb. beef chuck roast, cut into
    several large pieces
2 t. garlic, minced
1 t. ground cumin
1 t. chili powder
1 t. salt
1 t. pepper
14-1/2 oz. can diced tomatoes
    with onion and garlic
8-oz. can hot or plain tomato
    sauce
1/2 c. water
2 T. vinegar
3 bay leaves

Arrange green pepper and onion slices in a slow cooker. Top with beef; sprinkle with garlic and seasonings. Pour undrained tomatoes, tomato sauce, water and vinegar over beef; add bay leaves. Push beef down until mostly covered by tomato mixture. Cover and cook on low setting for 6 to 8 hours, until beef can be shredded easily. Shred beef using 2 forks; discard bay leaves. Keep warm in slow cooker until ready to serve. Serves 6 to 8.

If you love super-spicy chili, give New Mexico chili powder a try. Sold at Hispanic and specialty food stores, it contains pure ground red chili peppers, unlike regular chili powder, which is a blend of chili peppers, garlic and other seasonings.

59

Tamale Pie Casserole

Tracie Williams
Carrollton, TX

This is a delicious comfort meal that my family enjoys. It is
so quick to prepare...just toss it all together and pop it in the oven.
Before you know it, dinner is served!

2 15-oz. cans beef tamales,
  unwrapped and cut into
  1-inch pieces
15-oz. can tomato sauce
14-3/4 oz. can creamed corn
10-oz. can diced tomatoes with
  green chiles
4-1/4 oz. can chopped black
  olives, drained

4-oz. can chopped green chiles,
  drained
1/2 c. banana pepper rings,
  chopped
8-oz. pkg. shredded sharp
  Cheddar cheese
1 c. tortilla chips, crushed

In a greased 2-1/2 quart casserole dish, mix together all ingredients
except tortilla chips. Bake, uncovered, at 350 degrees for 45 to
50 minutes, until hot and bubbly. Top with crushed chips just before
serving. Makes 6 servings.

The secret to serving a hearty homestyle casserole on a busy
weeknight! Simply prepare a favorite casserole recipe the night
before, cover and refrigerate. Just add 15 to 20 extra minutes
to the baking time.

Tuesday is Tex-Mex Night

Megan's Crazy Spicy Chili

Megan Sabo
Daytona Beach, FL

Mom gave me this easy chili recipe when I was learning to cook.
After I'd made it for awhile, I decided to add a couple of things
and now I have a spicy new version that's my very own.

1 lb. ground beef
1 onion, chopped
1/2 lb. spicy ground pork
   sausage
1/2 lb. andouille pork link
   sausage, sliced
2 15-1/2 oz. cans red kidney
   beans
2 14-1/2 oz. cans diced
   tomatoes

2 8-oz. cans tomato sauce
1 c. frozen corn
1-1/2 c. water
1-1/4 oz. pkg. chili seasoning
   mix
Garnish: sour cream, shredded
   Cheddar cheese, corn chips

In a large soup pot over medium-high heat, brown beef and onion;
drain and set aside in a bowl. In the same pot, brown spicy sausage
and andouille together; drain. Add beef mixture, undrained beans,
undrained tomatoes and remaining ingredients except garnish. Reduce
heat to low and simmer for about one hour, stirring occasionally. Serve
in individual bowls topped with sour cream, cheese and corn chips.
Serves 6 to 8.

If you can't stand the heat, get out of the kitchen!

– Harry S. Truman

Tex-Mex Zucchini Skillet

Judy Henfey
Cibolo, TX

My sister-in-law Jane first made this recipe over 20 years ago for a barbecue. It's a fast, easy side dish that goes great with chicken or beef. Enjoy!

2 T. olive oil
4 c. zucchini, thinly sliced
3/4 c. celery, chopped
1/2 c. onion, chopped
1/2 c. red or green pepper, sliced
1/2 c. hot or mild picante sauce

1-1/2 t. dried basil
1 t. salt
pepper to taste
1 c. shredded Monterey Jack
   cheese

Heat olive oil in a large skillet over high heat; add vegetables. Sauté for 3 minutes, stirring frequently. Add picante sauce and seasonings; stir well. Cover and cook for 3 to 5 minutes, until vegetables are tender. Remove from heat. Add cheese; mix well and let stand for a few minutes, until cheese is just melted. Makes 4 to 6 servings.

If you have a bumper crop of green, yellow or red peppers, freeze them whole...it's simple! Just wash well, slice off the tops and remove the seeds. Wrap peppers individually in aluminum foil and place in a freezer bag. Peppers can be sliced or chopped while still slightly frozen.

Lisa's Chicken Taco Salad

Lisa Sett
Thousand Oaks, CA

*A quick-to-fix hearty salad for a summer dinner. Make it
even quicker with already-grilled chicken strips.*

1 T. oil
1 lb. boneless, skinless chicken
  breasts, cut into strips
1 T. chili powder, or to taste
16-oz. pkg. salad greens or
  romaine lettuce
1 c. shredded Cheddar cheese
15-1/2 oz. can kidney beans,
  drained and rinsed

1/4 c. ranch salad dressing
1/4 c. salsa
Garnish: crushed tortilla chips
Optional: sliced avocado,
  chopped tomatoes, sliced
  black olives, chopped fresh
  cilantro

Heat oil in a large non-stick skillet over medium heat. Sprinkle chicken
strips with chili powder. Cook chicken in oil for about 8 minutes, until
golden on all sides and cooked through; drain. Combine greens or
lettuce, chicken, cheese, beans, salad dressing and salsa in a large
serving bowl; toss to mix. Top with crushed chips; add optional
toppings as desired. Makes 6 servings.

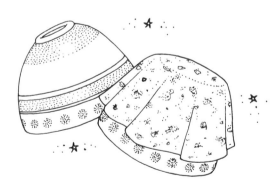

Kids big and small will love tortilla bowls filled with a crisp,
crunchy salad! Spray one side of a tortilla and the outside of an
oven-safe bowl with non-stick vegetable spray. Place the tortilla
over the bowl, oiled-side up. Bake at 350 degrees for 15 minutes
or until golden; let cool before filling.

Homemade Indian Tacos

Crystal Branstrom
Russell, PA

*My family can hardly wait for dinner to be served when
Indian Tacos are on the menu!*

1 lb. ground beef
1-1/4 oz. pkg. taco seasoning
  mix
16-oz. can refried beans

Garnish: shredded Cheddar
  cheese, shredded lettuce,
  chopped tomatoes, salsa,
  sour cream, guacamole

Brown beef in a skillet over medium heat; drain. Stir in seasoning and
beans; cover and keep warm while making Fry Bread. To serve, spread
beef mixture over warm Fry Bread; top with garnishes of your choice.
Makes 4 to 6 servings.

Fry Bread:

2 c. all-purpose flour
1/4 c. sugar
1 t. baking powder

1 t. salt
1 c. water
oil for deep frying

In a bowl, mix together flour, sugar, baking powder and salt. Stir in
enough water to make a soft dough. Divide dough into 4 to 6 portions.
On a floured surface, pat each portion into a circle, about one inch
thick. In a deep skillet over medium-high heat, heat one to 2 inches of
oil to 350 degrees. Fry dough circles, one at a time, until golden on
both sides. Drain on paper towels.

Paper coffee filters make tidy holders for tacos or
sandwich wraps...easy for little hands to hold too.

Dinnertime Nachos

Michelle Corriveau
Blackstone, MA

*This simple recipe pleases even the fussiest eaters. You can add
your favorite toppings to make it special. Try adding some
smoky-flavored BBQ sauce to the taco meat...yum!*

1 lb. lean ground beef
1-1/4 oz. pkg. taco seasoning
   mix
1-1/2 c. skim milk
2 T. all-purpose flour
1-1/2 to 2 c. shredded Cheddar-
   Jack cheese

6-oz. pkg. tortilla chips
Garnish: shredded lettuce,
   chopped tomatoes
Optional: sour cream

Brown beef in a skillet over medium heat. Drain; stir in taco seasoning
and cover to keep warm. In a separate saucepan over medium heat,
combine milk and flour; whisk well. Cook and stir over medium heat
until mixture thickens and comes to a slow boil. Remove from heat.
Add cheese to milk mixture; stir until cheese is melted. Layer 4 dinner
plates with tortilla chips. Top with cheese sauce, beef mixture, lettuce,
tomatoes and a dollop of sour cream, if desired. Makes 4 servings.

Hot, hot, hot! If a dish proves just too spicy for
your taste, reach for a glass of milk, not water...
it's much better for cooling the heat. Nibbling
on a flour tortilla or a slice of bread
may help quench the flames too.

Aurora's Chicken Taquitos

Gayla Reyes
Hamilton, OH

My husband was born in Mexico. His mom, who still lives there, explained to him over the phone how to teach me to cook these. They are now a family favorite! They are messy but so yummy...have lots of napkins handy! If you have a local Mexican tienda (grocery store) they will have everything you need, but I've included some supermarket substitutions too.

30 6-inch corn tortillas
3-lb. deli roast chicken,
   shredded
1/2 c. corn oil
8-oz. container Mexican crema
   or sour cream

16-oz. jar salsa
3 c. lettuce, chopped
16-oz. pkg. crumbled queso
   fresco or shredded Monterey
   Jack cheese

In a large skillet over medium heat, warm tortillas, 3 to 4 at a time, until soft and easy to handle. Flip tortillas after 3 minutes; remove from skillet. Add 2 tablespoons of shredded chicken to half of each tortilla. Roll up tightly; place seam-side down in a large dish. When all taquitos have been rolled, add oil to skillet and heat over medium-high heat. When oil is hot, carefully add taquitos, seam-side down, until skillet is full. Fry for about 5 minutes; turn taquitos over with tongs and fry on other side for 5 minutes, until golden. To eat, pick up a taquito with your fingers and top with crema or sour cream, salsa, lettuce and cheese. Serves 6 to 8.

Set out stacks of colorful bandannas...they make super-size fun napkins when enjoying tacos, fajitas and other messy food!

Tuesday is Tex-Mex Night

West Texas Party Drumsticks

Louise Graybiel
Ontario, Canada

A crunchy alternative to traditional chicken wings.

1 c. ranch salad dressing
1 T. hot pepper sauce
1 c. corn flake cereal, finely
    crushed

1-1/4 oz. pkg. taco seasoning
    mix
12 chicken drumsticks

In a shallow dish, combine salad dressing and hot sauce. In a separate dish or a plastic zipping bag, combine cereal and taco seasoning. Dip drumsticks in salad dressing mixture; coat well with cereal mixture. Arrange in a greased 13"x9" baking pan. Bake, uncovered, at 350 degrees for one hour, or until juices run clear. Serves 4 to 6.

Secret-Ingredient Mexican Beef

Diana Krol
Nickerson, KS

My kids love Mexican food, but are convinced that they don't like beans. This recipe allows me to stretch the beef and add nutrition without anyone being the wiser! I often multiply it for a large group and serve it out of a slow cooker set on low. It's terrific for fixing burritos, nachos and Mexican pizza.

1 lb. ground beef
16-oz. can pinto beans

2 T. taco seasoning mix

Brown beef in a skillet over medium heat; drain well. In a blender, purée beans and their liquid to a smooth consistency. In a microwave-safe container, stir beef, puréed beans and taco seasoning together. Cover; microwave on high setting until heated through. Serve as desired. Serves 6 to 8.

Jazz up good ol' stuffed peppers. Fill green peppers with Secret-Ingredient Mexican Beef, dollop with salsa and bake as usual. Serve with shredded cheese and other favorite toppings.

Dad's Mixed-Up Taco Salad

Tamara Underhill Richards
Somerset, CA

My hubby created this taco salad for our four sons...it's scrumptious. He combined all of their favorite taco fixin's into one absolutely huge bowl, and then, to our surprise, proceeded to mix it up with his hands. It's now a family favorite, and he still mixes it with his hands! Serve with tortillas and fresh fruit.

1 lb. lean ground beef
1-1/4 oz. pkg. taco seasoning
   mix
16-oz. pkg. salad mix
2 tomatoes, chopped
4-1/4 oz. can sliced black olives,
   drained
2 green onions, sliced
13-oz. pkg. nacho cheese-
   flavored tortilla chips

16-oz. pkg. shredded Cheddar or
   Monterey Jack cheese
Garnishes: sour cream,
   guacamole or cubed avocado,
   sliced jalapeño peppers,
   black beans, corn, salsa,
   ranch salad dressing

In a skillet over medium heat, brown beef until no longer pink. Add taco seasoning according to package directions; set aside. In a very large bowl, combine salad mix, tomatoes, olives and onions. Crush tortilla chips before opening bag. Add chips and cheese to mixture in bowl; toss with your hands. Add beef mixture; toss again until all ingredients are evenly distributed. Serve with desired toppings. Serves 6.

Hosting a party for family & friends? Make it a potluck with a twist. You provide a hearty main course like enchilada casserole... invite others to bring their own specialties like tossed salads, veggie dishes, yeast rolls and so on. Less work and more fun for everyone!

Mexican Chicken Chili

Beth Smith
Manchester, MI

My sister-in-law Penny made this slow-cooker stew for a gathering and it has become my son Nathan's favorite soup.

3 to 4 boneless, skinless chicken breasts
2 15-oz. cans Great Northern beans, drained
15-oz. can hominy, drained
4-oz. can chopped green chiles
10-3/4 oz. can low-sodium cream of mushroom soup
1-1/4 oz. pkg. taco seasoning mix
Optional: milk or chicken broth
Garnish: diced green onion, nacho cheese-flavored tortilla chips

Place chicken in a 4-quart slow cooker. Layer with beans, hominy, chiles and soup; sprinkle taco seasoning over top. Cover and cook on low setting for 7 to 8 hours. Do not peek and do not stir during cooking. At serving time, use a spoon to break up chicken; stir. If chili is too thick, add a little milk or broth to desired consistency. Garnish with diced green onion. Serve with tortilla chips. Makes 6 servings.

Crunchy tortilla strips are tasty toppers for southwestern-style soups. Cut corn tortillas into thin strips, then deep-fry quickly and drain on paper towels. Try red or blue tortillas for variety.

Pueblo-Style Beef Tacos

Suzn Reazin
Albuquerque, NM

My husband taught me how to make these tacos after we were married. He said this was how his mother always made them and she was from Pueblo, Colorado. These are messy to eat...but oh-so good!

1-1/2 lbs. ground beef
15-oz. can pork & beans
6 cherry peppers, chopped
2 to 3 t. butter
8 to 10 6-inch corn tortillas
8-oz. pkg. shredded Cheddar
    cheese

Garnish: salsa, shredded lettuce,
    diced tomatoes
Optional: sliced avocado, black
    olives

Brown beef in a skillet over medium heat; drain. Stir in pork & beans and peppers; heat until warmed through. Meanwhile, melt butter in a small skillet over medium heat; warm tortillas in the skillet on both sides until soft. To serve, fill each tortilla with 2 tablespoons of beef mixture. Top with cheese, salsa, lettuce and tomatoes. Serve with avocado and black olives, if desired. Serves 4 to 5.

When the summertime garden is bursting with tomatoes, peppers and onions, make homemade salsa...it's a snap. Process veggies in a blender, add some fresh cilantro, salt and lime juice. You can't go wrong... adjust the amounts to suit your own taste.

Lil's Fiesta Cornbread

Lillian Child
Omaha, NE

I've been making this cornbread since I was first introduced to Mexican food by a Latino friend of mine many years ago. This is a favorite, as it adds a bit of sweetness to help cool the spicy Mexican dishes we enjoy it with.

8-1/2 oz. pkg. corn muffin mix
1/2 c. butter, melted and cooled
  slightly
8-oz. container sour cream
2 eggs, lightly beaten
14-3/4 oz. can creamed corn
15-oz. can shoepeg corn,
  drained
11-oz. can sweet corn and diced
  peppers, drained
4-oz. can chopped green chiles,
  drained
1 c. shredded Mexican-blend
  cheese

Combine dry corn muffin mix and remaining ingredients in a large bowl; stir just until moistened. Spray a 2-quart casserole dish with non-stick vegetable spray. Pour batter into dish. Bake at 375 degrees for one hour, or until golden and center is set. Let stand about 20 minutes to allow cornbread to set up. Makes 8 to 10 servings.

Nothing goes better with hearty Mexican flavors than warm cornbread! Bake it in a vintage cast-iron skillet...the cornbread will bake up with a crisp golden crust.

Fiesta Chili Pie Pronto

Sue Klapper
Muskego, WI

This speedy recipe makes dinnertime party time
for my family and me!

8-1/2 oz. pkg. corn muffin mix
1 egg, lightly beaten
1/3 c. milk
15-oz. can chili without beans
8-oz. pkg. shredded Cheddar
    Jack cheese

1/4 c. chopped black olives
Optional: chopped tomatoes,
    sour cream

Lightly spray a 10" round flan or springform pan with non-stick vegetable spray. Line the bottom of pan with a circle of parchment paper cut to fit; set aside. In a bowl, combine dry corn muffin mix, egg and milk; stir until well blended. Pour batter into pan. Bake at 350 degrees for 20 minutes, or until lightly golden. Cool crust in pan on a wire rack for 10 minutes; turn out onto a serving plate. Peel off paper. Heat or microwave chili until hot; pour chili over crust. Top with cheese and olives; add tomatoes and sour cream, if desired. Cut into wedges. Makes 8 servings.

Need a box of corn muffin mix and don't have one in the pantry? Here's a quick substitution: 1-1/4 cups yellow cornmeal, one cup all-purpose flour, 1/2 cup sugar, 4 teaspoons baking powder and 1/2 teaspoon salt. Use in place of an 8-1/2 ounce package.

Cheesy Chicken Quesadillas

Becky Badilla
Great Mills, MD

Whenever our family went out to eat Mexican food, someone always ordered the chicken quesadillas. So I decided to come up with my own version to make at home. This is simple, and the kids love it.

1 T. olive oil	1 c. picante sauce
1-1/2 lbs. boneless, skinless chicken breasts, cubed	6 8-inch flour tortillas
Optional: salt and pepper to taste	6 slices Colby Jack cheese
1 to 2 T. taco seasoning mix	6 slices Pepper Jack cheese
	Garnish: sour cream

Heat oil in a skillet over medium heat. Add chicken; season with salt and pepper, if desired. Cook chicken until no longer pink; drain. Stir in taco seasoning and picante sauce; cook over low heat until warmed through. Layer each tortilla with one slice of Colby Jack cheese, a spoonful of chicken mixture and one slice of Pepper Jack cheese. Fold tortillas in half; arrange on a baking sheet. Bake at 425 degrees for 5 to 10 minutes, turning once, until crisp and golden. Serve with sour cream. Makes 6 servings.

Whenever you're grilling chicken for dinner, toss a few extra boneless, skinless chicken breasts on the grill. Sliced and refrigerated, they can be served another day in quesadillas, tacos or burritos for an easy meal with fresh-grilled flavor.

Quick Quesadilla for One

Mary Weldon
Fremont, NE

When I make this tasty recipe for my family & friends, everyone is astonished how fast it is ready to go in the oven...less than five minutes! If I fix my own chicken, I can cook up a lot with the fajita seasoning and freeze it, handy for making quick meals. No one leaves the table hungry!

2 8-inch flour tortillas
1 T. ranch salad dressing,
    divided
1/2 c. fajita-seasoned cooked
    chicken, diced

1/2 c. shredded mozzarella
    cheese

Spread one side of each tortilla with 1-1/2 teaspoons salad dressing. Top one tortilla with chicken, cheese and remaining tortilla, dressing-side down. Place on an aluminum foil-lined, lightly greased baking sheet. Bake at 350 degrees for 20 minutes, or until as crisp as desired. Cut into wedges. Serves one.

Mother's Sour Cream Rice

Autumn Jimenez
Fresno, CA

When I was growing up, my mother brought a double batch of this recipe to almost all of our church potlucks. It's a great recipe to use up leftover cooked rice...tastes great served alongside enchiladas!

2 to 2-1/2 c. cooked rice
4-oz. can diced green chiles
8-oz. pkg. shredded Cheddar or
    Monterey Jack cheese

16-oz. container sour cream
salt and pepper to taste

Combine all ingredients in a bowl; stir well. Spoon mixture into a buttered 2-quart casserole dish. Bake, uncovered, at 350 degrees for 30 minutes, or until hot and bubbly. Serves 6 to 8.

Make your pizza cutter do double duty! It's handy for cutting quesadillas into wedges...terrific for slicing tortillas into strips too.

South-of-the-Border Rice

Nichole Martelli
Santa Fe, TX

*Who needs a packaged mix when this seasoned rice
is so simple to stir up?*

2 T. olive oil
2 c. long-cooking rice, uncooked
1 c. salsa or tomato sauce
1 t. garlic, minced
1 t. chili powder

1 t. ground cumin
1/4 t. salt
1/2 t. pepper
4 c. water

In a saucepan, heat oil over medium heat. Add rice; cook and stir until rice is lightly golden. Stir in remaining ingredients; reduce heat to low. Cover and cook for about 20 minutes, until rice is tender. Serves 4.

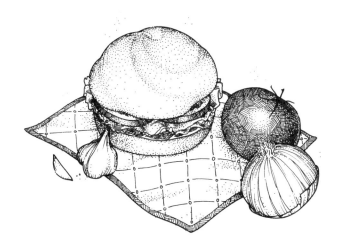

It's easy to give a Tex-Mex twist to your favorite dishes. Serve burgers topped with Pepper Jack cheese and salsa, with Mexican rice on the side. Hankering for pizza? Layer ready-to-bake pizza crusts with browned and seasoned beef, sautéed sweet peppers, diced tomatoes and Mexican-blend cheese. It's cook's choice!

Hearty Spanish Rice

Michelle Tallman
Lacey, WA

*A great way to use up a leftover roast! My family has
loved this dish for a long time.*

14-1/2 oz. can Mexican-style
   stewed tomatoes
3/4 c. quick-cooking brown rice,
   uncooked
2/3 c. water
1/2 t. sugar
1/4 t. garlic powder
1/4 t. pepper
1/2 c. salsa

15-oz. can black beans, drained
   and rinsed
1 to 1-1/4 c. cooked beef, pork
   or chicken, chopped
6 to 8 8-inch flour tortillas
Garnish: shredded Cheddar
   cheese, salsa, sour cream,
   guacamole

In a large skillet, stir together undrained tomatoes, rice, water, sugar
and seasonings. Bring to a boil over medium-high heat. Reduce heat to
low; cover and simmer for about 12 to 15 minutes, until rice is tender.
Stir in salsa, beans and meat; heat through. To serve, spoon mixture
into warmed tortillas; add your favorite toppings. Serves 6.

A fresh-tasting chopped salad of
lettuce and tomatoes is always
welcome alongside spicy Mexican
dishes. Try this easy dressing. In a
covered jar, combine 3 tablespoons
olive oil, 2 tablespoons lime juice,
1/4 teaspoon dry mustard and
1/2 teaspoon salt. Cover and
shake until well blended.

Skillet Turkey Tacos

Maria Kuhns
Crofton, MD

A hearty, healthy alternative to traditional tacos. It's an easy dinner for weeknights, or in the summertime when you just don't want to turn on the oven!

2 c. elbow macaroni, uncooked
1 lb. ground turkey
1/2 c. onion, chopped
1/2 c. green pepper, chopped
4 8-oz. cans tomato sauce
1/2 c. picante sauce
1 to 2 c. baked tortilla chips, crushed
1 to 2 c. shredded lettuce

1 c. shredded low-fat Cheddar or Mexican-blend cheese
Garnish: low-fat sour cream, chopped avocado, sliced black olives, sliced jalapeño peppers
Optional: additional picante sauce

Cook macaroni according to package directions; drain. Meanwhile, spray a skillet with non-stick vegetable spray. Over medium heat, brown turkey with onion and green pepper until turkey is no longer pink; drain. Add sauces and cooked macaroni; bring to a boil. Reduce heat to low. Simmer about 10 minutes. Divide crushed chips among 4 dinner plates; top with turkey mixture, lettuce and cheese. Add toppings; drizzle with more picante sauce for extra heat, if desired. Serves 4.

Whimsical vintage salt & pepper shakers add a dash of fun at mealtime. Look for them at flea markets or thrift shops...you're sure to find some favorites.

Santa Fe Chicken & Potatoes

Tina George
El Dorado, AR

This five-ingredient recipe is simple to prepare on busy nights when you're pressed for time! It smells so good when it's cooking, and it's easy to double for my large family. My family loves this dish served with sweet cornbread muffins.

4 potatoes, peeled and cut into 3/4-inch cubes
1 lb. boneless, skinless chicken breasts, cut into 3/4-inch cubes

2 T. olive oil
1 c. salsa
11-oz. can corn, drained

Place potatoes in a microwave-safe dish; add a small amount of water. Cover with plastic wrap; vent and microwave on high for 8 to 10 minutes, until tender. Meanwhile, in a large skillet over high heat, sauté chicken in oil over medium-high heat for 5 minutes. Add potatoes; sauté and toss until potatoes are lightly golden. Stir in salsa and corn; toss until heated through. Serves 4.

A muffin tin is handy when you're serving lots of tasty toppings. Fill up the sections with shredded cheese, guacamole, diced tomatoes and sour cream...and let everyone mix & match their favorites!

Tuesday is **Tex-Mex Night**

Chicken Tortilla Soup

Heidi Heisterkamp
Fort Wayne, IN

Talk about a "wow" soup! I've often made this slow-cooker soup for easy weeknight meals and tailgating parties too. The compliments are sky-high, even though it's the easiest meal to prepare.

4 boneless, skinless chicken
    breasts
2 15-oz. cans Mexican-style
    stewed tomatoes
4-oz. can chopped green chiles
2 15-oz. cans black beans

15-oz. can tomato sauce
1 c. salsa
tortilla chips
Garnish: shredded Cheddar
    cheese

Place chicken in a slow cooker. In a bowl, mix undrained tomatoes, chiles and beans. Stir in sauce and salsa; spoon over chicken. Cover and cook on low setting for 8 hours. Just before serving, remove chicken and cut into bite-sized pieces; stir back into mixture in slow cooker. To serve, line soup bowls with tortilla chips. Ladle soup over chips and top with cheese. Serves 6 to 8.

Welcoming extra guests for dinner? It's easy to stretch a pot of soup to make more servings...just add an extra can or two of tomatoes or beans. The soup will be extra hearty, and no one will know the difference!

Shrimp Soft Tacos

Shirl Parsons
Cape Carteret, NC

A light tropical-inspired meal that can be prepared in no time...delicious!

1 c. yellow peppers, sliced
1 c. red onion, sliced
1 clove garlic, minced
1-1/2 lbs. medium shrimp,
    cleaned
1 c. tomatoes, chopped

1/2 t. ground cumin
1/2 t. chili powder
2 T. fresh cilantro, chopped
8 6-inch flour tortillas
1-1/4 c. shredded low-fat
    Monterey Jack cheese

Spray a skillet with non-stick vegetable spray. Over medium-high heat, sauté pepper, onion and garlic for 2 minutes. Add shrimp, tomatoes and seasonings; sauté for 3 minutes, or until shrimp are no longer pink. Stir in cilantro. Top each tortilla with 1/4 cup shrimp mixture, 3 tablespoons cheese and 2 tablespoons Tropical Salsa; fold over. Makes 8 servings.

Tropical Salsa:

11-oz. can mandarin oranges,
    drained
8-oz. can pineapple tidbits,
    drained

1/4 c. green onions, chopped
1 T. chopped green chiles
1 T. fresh cilantro, chopped
1 T. lemon juice

Mix all ingredients in a bowl; cover and chill.

Puff-pastry shells are a tasty change from tortillas. Thaw a 10-ounce package of frozen puff pastry, roll it out and cut into circles. Bake at 400 degrees for 15 minutes, or until crisp and golden.

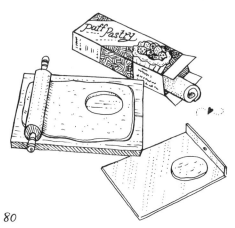

Light & Healthy Fish Tacos

Cherie Dominguez
Tumwater, WA

A quick & easy low-fat meal you're sure to love. One fish fillet will usually make a serving of two tacos. If you like, leave out the jalapeño pepper in the salsa...it can be served on the side for those with braver taste buds.

4 fillets mahi-mahi, halibut or
    other mild white fish
4 to 8 6-inch flour tortillas

Garnish: shredded Cheddar Jack
    cheese, shredded cabbage
1 lime, cut into wedges

Grill fish as desired. When fish is cooked through, slice each fillet into 2 long pieces. Warm tortillas in a skillet. To serve, fill each tortilla with a piece of fish, some cheese and some cabbage. Top with Fresh Tomato Salsa and a squeeze of lime juice. Serves 4.

Fresh Tomato Salsa:

2 tomatoes, diced
2 to 3 T. fresh cilantro, chopped
garlic salt to taste

Optional: 1 t. jalapeño pepper,
    finely diced

Combine tomatoes and cilantro; add garlic salt to taste. Add jalapeño pepper, if using; mix gently. Cover and chill.

Sugar the rim of glasses before filling with iced tea or lemonade. Run a lemon wedge around the rim and place the glass upside-down in a small plate of sugar. Tap off any extra sugar before filling.

Easy Enchilada Casserole

Lauren Williams
Kewanee, MO

We love this casserole...it combines so many textures and flavors!
Top it with sour cream and salsa for a southwestern-style feast.

2 lbs. ground beef
1 onion, chopped
10-oz. can enchilada sauce
10-3/4 oz. can cream of
  mushroom soup

10-3/4 oz. can cream of chicken
  soup
16-oz. pkg. shredded Cheddar
  cheese
6-oz. pkg. corn chips

In a large skillet over medium heat, brown beef and onion; drain well.
Stir in sauce and soups. Transfer beef mixture to a lightly greased
13"x9" baking pan; top with cheese and corn chips. Bake, uncovered,
at 350 degrees for 45 minutes, or until hot and bubbly. Makes
8 servings.

Busy-Night Taco Bake

Sharon Murray
Lexington Park, MD

It only takes about 30 minutes to whip up this hearty dish!

1 lb. ground beef
1-1/4 oz. pkg. taco seasoning
  mix
3/4 c. water

6 6-inch flour tortillas
2 c. shredded Mexican-blend or
  Cheddar cheese, divided
1 to 2 c. salsa

Brown beef in a skillet over medium heat; drain. Stir in taco seasoning
and water; simmer for 5 minutes. Cover the bottom of a lightly greased
9"x9" baking pan with 3 tortillas. Top with one cup cheese and all of
beef mixture. Layer with remaining tortillas, salsa and 1/2 cup cheese.
Bake, uncovered, at 350 degrees for 15 minutes. Top with remaining
cheese. Bake for an additional 5 to 10 minutes, until bubbly and
cheese is melted. Serves 4.

Tuesday is Tex-Mex Night

Chili Verde Pork

Charlene McCain
Bakersfield, CA

We love slow-cooked pork with green chiles in our tacos and burritos!
The kids just fill a cold flour tortilla and off they run. I like mine
tostada style, layering a fried tortilla with warmed refried beans, chili
verde and tomato, lettuce, olives and sour cream on top. This makes
a lot, but leftovers can be frozen for up to two months.

2-1/2 to 3-lb. boneless pork
    roast, cut into large cubes
1/2 c. all-purpose flour
1/4 c. oil

1 onion, diced
7-oz. can chopped green chiles
14-1/2 oz. can chicken broth

Coat pork cubes with flour; shake off excess. Heat oil in a deep skillet
over medium-high heat. Brown pork cubes on all sides; drain. Add
remaining ingredients. Reduce heat to low; cover and simmer about
30 minutes. Transfer mixture to a slow cooker. Cover and cook on low
setting for 6 to 8 hours, until pork is very tender. Serve as desired.
Serves 6 to 8.

So-Good New Mexico Salsa

Bobbie Chavez
Rio Rancho, NM

This flavorful salsa is a staple at our house. It's delicious in tacos,
egg dishes and burritos, and as a dip for tortilla chips.

28-oz. can whole tomatoes
1/2 onion, chopped
2 jalapeño peppers, seeded
    and chopped

2 cloves garlic, finely chopped
1 to 2 T. dried pequin peppers,
    crushed, or red pepper flakes
salt to taste

Pour undrained tomatoes into a blender. Add remaining ingredients
except salt; pulse to desired consistency. Add salt to taste. Transfer
salsa to a one-quart wide-mouth canning jar or other covered
container; keep refrigerated. Makes about 4 cups.

Easy Beef & Tater Burritos

Cathie Lopez
La Mirada, CA

My mom used to make these burritos for lunch or dinner...I still enjoy them! Add your favorite salsa for a spicy treat.

1 lb. ground beef
2 russet potatoes, peeled and
 diced
2 T. olive oil
1/2 red or white onion, chopped
salt, pepper and garlic powder to
 taste

Optional: red pepper flakes to
 taste
6 10-inch flour or corn tortillas
Garnish: shredded Cheddar
 cheese, sour cream, other
 favorite toppings

Brown beef in a skillet over medium heat; drain and set aside. Meanwhile, place potatoes in a microwave-safe dish; add a small amount of water. Cover with plastic wrap; vent and microwave on high for 8 to 10 minutes, until tender. Add oil, onion and potatoes to skillet; cook until tender and golden. Return beef to skillet; add seasonings to taste. To serve, spoon mixture onto tortillas. Roll into burritos, adding cheese, sour cream and other desired toppings. Serves 6.

Spice up your favorite ranch salad dressing. To one cup dressing, whisk in 1/2 teaspoon ground cumin and 1/4 teaspoon chili powder. Let stand a few minutes so the flavors can blend.

Mexicali Meatloaf

Vickie
Gooseberry Patch

Treat your family to juicy slices of this flavorful meatloaf!
It's a great use for a few extra corn muffins too.

1-1/2 lbs. ground beef
1/2 lb. ground pork
1/2 c. cornbread, crumbled
1/4 c. milk
1 egg, beaten
1/2 c. sour cream
1/2 c. shredded Pepper Jack
   cheese

3/4 c. corn
1/2 c. onion, minced
3 to 4 jalapeño peppers, seeded
   and chopped
2 cloves garlic, minced
1 t. salt
1 t. pepper

Mix together beef and pork gently in a large bowl; set aside. In a separate bowl, combine remaining ingredients; mix well. Gently stir cornbread mixture into beef mixture. Form into a rounded loaf; place in a lightly greased 2-quart casserole dish. Bake, uncovered, at 350 degrees for 45 minutes. Cover loosely with aluminum foil; return to oven for an additional 10 to 15 minutes. Let stand several minutes before slicing. Makes 8 servings.

Fresh hot peppers from your own garden or a nearby farmers' market are extra flavorful, but take care when slicing them. It's best to wear rubber gloves, and be sure not to touch your eyes!

Spencer's Corn Chip Casserole

Carol Hickman
Kingsport, TN

A local drive-in restaurant serves a corn chip tortilla wrap that my son Spencer just loves. He asked me to create a casserole that tastes like it. This recipe is what I came up with...my family gives it two thumbs up!

1 lb. lean ground beef
2/3 c. red onion, finely diced
15-oz. can chili-style diced
   tomatoes
16-oz. can chili beans
8-oz. can tomato sauce
1-1/4 oz. pkg. chili seasoning
   mix

6 to 8 8-inch flour tortillas
3 c. corn chips, lightly crushed
3 c. finely shredded Mexican-
   blend cheese
Garnish: sour cream, diced
   green onions, sliced jalapeño
   peppers

In a large saucepan over medium heat, brown beef and onion; drain. Add undrained tomatoes, undrained beans, sauce and seasoning; stir well. Simmer over medium heat until heated through; remove from heat. Lightly spray a 13"x9" baking pan with non-stick vegetable spray. Layer 3 to 4 tortillas to cover the bottom of pan; overlap and halve tortillas, if necessary. Spread half of beef mixture over tortillas; sprinkle evenly with half of corn chips and half of cheese. Repeat layers, ending with cheese. Bake, uncovered, at 350 degrees for 30 minutes, or until bubbly and cheese is melted. Let stand several minutes before serving. Top individual servings with a dollop of sour cream, diced onions and jalapeño slices. Serves 6 to 8.

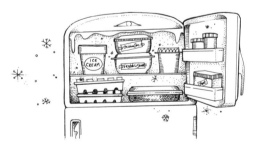

Fix a double batch! Brown two pounds of ground beef with two packages of taco seasoning mix, then freeze half of the mixture for a quick meal another night. What a time-saver!

Golden Sopapillas

*Kay Smith
LaJara, CO*

*Everyone loves these delicious little pillows of hot bread! Serve them
with honey butter or stuff with your favorite taco filling.*

1-3/4 c. all-purpose flour
2 t. baking powder
1 t. salt

2 T. shortening
2/3 c. cold water
oil for deep frying

In a bowl, mix flour, baking powder and salt. Cut in shortening with
a pastry cutter until mixture resembles cornmeal. Stir in water,
one tablespoon at a time, until a stiff dough forms; set aside. Add
4 inches of oil to a deep fryer; heat to about 400 degrees. While oil
heats, roll out dough on a floured surface until very thin. Cut into
4-inch squares. Test oil by dropping in a small piece of dough; if dough
browns quickly, it's ready. Fry each piece until it puffs up; turn over
carefully and fry until other side is golden. Lift out with a slotted
spoon; drain on paper towels. Serve warm. Makes one dozen.

Mix-Your-Own Taco Spice

*Josh Logan
Victoria, TX*

*If you enjoy Mexican food often, why not make your own seasoning
mix? Add or subtract ingredients to suit your family's taste.*

2 T. chili powder
1 T. ground cumin
2 t. salt
2 t. pepper
1 t. paprika

1/2 t. garlic powder
1/2 t. onion powder
1/2 t. dried oregano
1/2 t. red pepper flakes

In a small bowl, mix together all ingredients. Store in a small covered
jar. Makes about 1/3 cup.

Whip up a crock of honey butter to serve with warm sopapillas
or cornbread. Simply combine 1/2 cup softened butter
with 2/3 cup honey...yum!

"Deep-Fried" Ice Cream

Kathy Kehring
Scottsdale, AZ

Living here in the Southwest, my family loves the deep-fried
ice cream dessert served in Mexican restaurants. This recipe is
a quick & easy version of the real thing.

4 c. bite-size crispy cinnamon
rice cereal squares, lightly
crushed
1 c. mini semi-sweet chocolate
chips

2 pts. vanilla ice cream
1/2 lb. fresh strawberries, hulled
and sliced
Garnish: honey, whipped cream

Combine cereal and chocolate chips in a bowl; set aside. Scoop 8 balls
of ice cream with an ice cream scoop. Quickly roll ice cream balls in
cereal mixture; mound balls in a 9" pie plate. Cover; freeze at least one
hour until firm. At serving time, top ice cream balls with strawberries.
Drizzle with honey and dollop with whipped cream. Makes 8 servings.

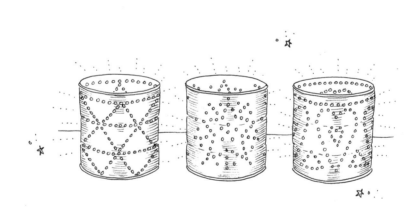

Pierced tin lanterns are so pretty twinkling on the dinner table.
Fill an empty tin can with water, freeze solid, then tap a design
of holes all around with awl and hammer. After the ice has
melted, set a votive candle inside.

Tim's Apple Burrito

Pat Gilmer
West Linn, OR

My husband Tim's mother taught him how to make this dessert when he was a boy. It's so simple...you'll love it too!

9-inch pie crust	1 T. all-purpose flour
2 c. apples, peeled, cored and chopped	1/2 t. cinnamon
	5 T. sugar, divided
2 T. raisins	1 T. butter, diced
2 T. chopped walnuts	2 t. water

Place pie crust on a baking sheet sprayed with non-stick vegetable spray. In a bowl, combine fruit, nuts, flour, cinnamon and 4 tablespoons sugar; toss to mix. Spoon mixture into the center of crust; dot with butter. Fold crust over; seal edges with a fork. Sprinkle crust with water and remaining sugar. Bake at 425 degrees for 20 to 25 minutes, until bubbly and golden. Serves 5 to 6.

Miss Add's Fruit Tacos

Cris Goode
Mooresville , IN

My daughter Addie just loves this fun twist on tacos!

4 10-inch flour tortillas	2 kiwis, peeled and sliced
1 c. fresh strawberries, hulled and sliced	Garnish: powdered sugar

Spray tortillas lightly on both sides with butter-flavored non-stick vegetable spray. In a skillet over medium-high heat, toast each tortilla on both sides. Divide fruit evenly among tortillas; fold over. Sprinkle lightly with powdered sugar. Serves 4.

A fresh, fun dessert that kids will love...fruit kabobs! Just slide juicy strawberries, pineapple chunks, kiwi fruit slices and orange sections onto wooden skewers.

Frozen Piña Colada Pie

Charlotte Smith
Tyrone, PA

Whenever I serve this light, refreshing pie, I know I won't have any leftovers! Not only is it scrumptious, it's easy to make ahead and tuck in the freezer for later.

8-oz. container frozen whipped
topping, thawed
3-oz. pkg. cream cheese,
softened
1 T. sugar
1/2 c. milk

8-oz. can crushed pineapple,
drained and divided
1-1/3 c. sweetened flaked
coconut
9-inch graham cracker crust

Spoon whipped topping into a bowl; set aside. In a blender, combine remaining ingredients except crust. Cover and process on medium speed for 30 seconds. Fold mixture into whipped topping; spoon into crust. Cover and freeze until firm, about 4 hours. Let stand 5 minutes at room temperature before slicing. Return any leftovers to the freezer. Serves 6 to 8.

When the weather is nice, carry dinner to the backyard for a picnic. You'll be making memories together...and just about everything seems to taste even better outdoors!

Stir-Fry Spaghetti

Christine Schnaufer
Geneseo, IL

This sauce is a favorite in the summer, a splendid fresh taste without long hours of cooking! It's delicious as a meatless sauce too...just omit the sausage and sauté the veggies in a little olive oil.

16-oz. pkg. spaghetti, uncooked
1 lb. Italian pork sausage links,
    cut into 1-inch slices
1 sweet onion, cut into 1/2-inch
    wedges
2 green peppers, cut into
    1/2-inch strips

4 to 5 tomatoes, cut into 1-inch
    wedges
1 to 2 cloves garlic, sliced
1 t. dried basil
1/2 t. dried oregano
salt and pepper to taste
8-oz. can tomato sauce

Cook spaghetti according to package directions; drain. Meanwhile, in a skillet over medium-high heat, cook sausage until lightly browned. Add onion, green peppers and tomatoes; cook and stir for 5 minutes. Add garlic and seasonings; stir and add tomato sauce. Reduce heat slightly; cook for 5 to 10 minutes. Serve over cooked spaghetti. Serves 6.

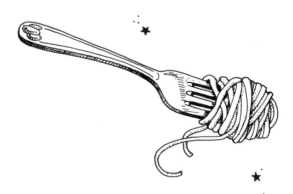

To cook up perfect pasta, fill a large pot with water (one gallon to one pound of pasta) and bring to a rolling boil. Add a tablespoon of salt, if desired. Stir in pasta; return to a rolling boil. Boil, uncovered, for the time recommended on package. There's no need to add oil...frequent stirring will keep pasta from sticking together.

Wednesday is **Italian Night**

Creamy Marinara Linguine

Sara Clepper
Boiling Springs, PA

When I make this dish for my family, they tell me they feel like they're dining in a wonderful Italian restaurant!

16-oz. pkg. linguine pasta, uncooked
2 cloves garlic, minced
1/4 c. olive oil
14-1/2 oz. can petite diced tomatoes

15-oz. jar Alfredo sauce
1/2 c. chicken broth or milk
1 t. dried Italian seasoning
1 t. dried parsley
salt and pepper to taste

Cook pasta according to package directions; drain. Meanwhile, in a skillet over medium heat, sauté garlic in olive oil for 30 seconds. Add undrained tomatoes; heat through. Add Alfredo sauce and chicken broth or milk. Stir until heated through; add seasonings. Serve over cooked pasta. Makes 4 servings.

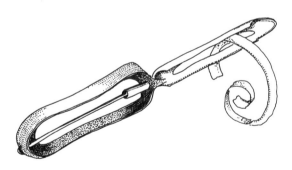

For a delicious, healthy change from regular pasta, make "noodles" from zucchini or summer squash. Cut the squash into long, thin strips, steam lightly or sauté in a little olive oil and toss with your favorite pasta sauce. Squash can also be sliced thinly, steamed and used instead of lasagna noodles. Give it a try!

Speedy Skillet Lasagna

Becky Butler
Keller, TX

Whenever I find oddly-shaped pasta, I like to use it in this dish. I've been known to break up regular lasagna noodles for this recipe too... it's even a nice way to use up a box with lots of broken pieces.

1 lb. lean ground beef
1/4 c. onion, chopped
1/2 c. carrot, peeled and chopped
1-1/2 c. mafalda mini lasagna
   noodles or other pasta,
   uncooked
1-1/2 c. water

2 c. marinara or other tomato-
   based pasta sauce
1/2 t. Italian seasoning
8-oz. pkg. sliced mushrooms
1/3 c. shredded mozzarella
   cheese, or more to taste

In a Dutch oven over medium-high heat, cook beef with onion and carrot for about 6 minutes, until beef is no longer pink. Drain. Stir in uncooked pasta and remaining ingredients except cheese. Heat to boiling, stirring occasionally. Reduce heat to low; simmer, uncovered, for 10 minutes, or until pasta is tender. Sprinkle with cheese before serving. Serves 6.

Make a favorite tomato-based spaghetti sauce thicker and richer!
Just stir in 6 tablespoons grated Parmesan cheese while
warming the sauce in a saucepan.

Sausage Penne Rosé

Lacey Lucas
New Brunswick, Canada

I've wowed guests many a time in less than 30 minutes with this recipe! It whips up in a jiffy and looks super fancy served with garlic bread and a crisp salad.

3 c. penne pasta, uncooked
2 to 3 t. olive oil
6 hot Italian pork sausage links,
    cut into 1/2-inch slices
2 c. rosé pasta sauce or creamy
    tomato pasta sauce

Optional: 1/2 c. cream cheese,
    softened
1 c. green, red and/or yellow
    peppers, thinly sliced

Cook pasta according to package directions, just until tender; drain. Meanwhile, heat oil in a large skillet over medium heat; cook sausages very well. Add pasta sauce and cream cheese, if using; reduce heat and simmer until warmed through. Add pepper strips and cook until crisp-tender. Toss with cooked pasta. Makes 4 servings.

Nothing perks up the flavor of tomato sauce like fresh basil!
Keep a pot of basil in the kitchen windowsill and just pinch off
a few leaves whenever they're needed.

Grandma's Sicilian Pizza

Nancy Julian
Alamogordo, NM

My grandmother made this hearty rustic pizza all the time. We would drive from Reno to San Jose to visit, and the smell of this pizza baking always greeted us. Dad would take the portion with anchovies...the rest of us were happy to let him have it! It's so quick to make, not much longer than having a pizza delivered.

14-1/2 oz. can stewed tomatoes
2 t. garlic, chopped
1 t. dried oregano
1 t. dried basil
2 c. shredded pizza-blend cheese

Garnish: chopped salami, olives, onions, green peppers, green chiles, other toppings
Optional: anchovies

Prepare Pizza Dough; let rise while preparing the sauce. In a saucepan over medium heat, combine undrained tomatoes, garlic and herbs. Bring to a boil; cook about 15 minutes, breaking up tomatoes with a spoon. Place Pizza Dough in the center of a greased 15"x10" jelly-roll pan; spread dough out to edges of pan. Spread sauce over dough; add cheese and desired toppings. Bake at 425 degrees for 30 to 40 minutes, until edges are lightly golden. Serves 4 to 6.

Pizza Dough:

1-1/3 c. warm water
1 env. active dry yeast
4 c. all-purpose flour

2 T. olive oil
1 t. salt

Heat water until very warm, about 110 to 115 degrees; pour into a large bowl. Add yeast; stir until dissolved. Add flour, olive oil and salt; mix well and let rise about 15 minutes.

For a crisp pizzeria-style finish, dust the pizza pan with cornmeal before adding the crust.

Leah's Italian Bread Pizza

Leah Beyer
Flat Rock, IN

My family really likes a hearty meat-topped pizza! So, I often buy Italian bread when it's marked down for quick sale. It's the start of this terrific thick-crust pizza that we all enjoy.

1 lb. ground pork, beef, turkey
   or chicken
1 t. Italian seasoning
1/2 t. garlic powder
1/2 t. salt
1/4 t. pepper
1 T. Worcestershire sauce

1/2 onion, diced
1/2 c. sliced mushrooms
1 c. cooked ham, cubed
15-oz. jar pizza sauce
1 loaf Italian bread, halved
   lengthwise
1 c. shredded mozzarella cheese

Brown meat in a skillet over medium heat; stir in seasonings and Worcestershire sauce as it cooks. Add onion and mushrooms; continue to cook just until vegetables are tender. Drain; add ham and heat through. Stir in pizza sauce. Place bread on an ungreased baking sheet, cut side up. Spoon meat mixture over bread; top with cheese. Bake at 350 degrees for 15 to 20 minutes, until golden and cheese is melted. Cut into slices. Makes 4 to 6 servings.

Keep your wooden cutting board in tip-top shape. Protect it from spills by coating with a thin film of olive oil and letting it soak in for a few minutes. Rub dry with a paper towel; repeat several times. Set the board aside for 24 hours before using again.

Simple Baked Mostaccioli

Michele Molen
Mendon, UT

*My Italian grandmother always used this quick & easy recipe when
she needed a dish for last-minute company or to send to a sick friend.
It will always be a comfort food to me...mangia, mangia!*

16-oz. pkg. mostaccioli pasta,
  uncooked
1 lb. ground beef
salt and pepper to taste

16-oz. jar pasta sauce, divided
16-oz. pkg. shredded mozzarella
  cheese, divided

Cook pasta according to package directions; drain. Meanwhile, brown
beef in a skillet over medium heat. Drain; season with salt and pepper.
Ladle a spoonful of pasta sauce into a greased 11"x8" glass baking
pan; add half of cooked pasta. Layer with all of beef mixture, half of
remaining sauce and half of cheese; repeat layers with remaining
pasta, sauce and cheese. Bake, uncovered, at 375 degrees for about
20 minutes, until hot and bubbly. Serves 5.

Caprese Salad

Beth Flack
Terre Haute, IN

*Very refreshing! This is one of my favorite summer salads. Try it
with cherry tomatoes and mini mozzarella balls too.*

2 beefsteak tomatoes, sliced
4-oz. pkg. fresh mozzarella
  cheese, sliced

8 leaves fresh basil
Italian salad dressing to taste

Layer tomatoes, cheese slices and basil leaves in a circle around a large
platter. Sprinkle with salad dressing. Cover and chill for one hour
before serving. Serves 6.

Meatball-Stuffed Shells

Jenny Bishoff
Mountain Lake Park, MD

As a working mom with two little girls, I've found this super-easy recipe is great for a quick dinner. The kids can help too!

12-oz. pkg. jumbo pasta shells, uncooked
28-oz. jar pasta sauce, divided

36 frozen Italian meatballs, thawed
2 c. shredded mozzarella cheese

Cook pasta according to package directions; drain and rinse in cold water. Spread 1/2 cup pasta sauce in a greased 13"x9" baking pan. Tuck a meatball into each shell; arrange shells in pan. Top with remaining sauce; add cheese. Cover; bake at 350 degrees for 35 minutes. Uncover and bake 10 more minutes. Serves 6 to 8.

Linda's Rigatoni Bake

Celia Day
Cerritos, CA

A dear friend made this yummy casserole for me years ago while I was recovering from surgery. Since then, I have been fixing it for my family...it's their favorite!

16-oz. pkg. rigatoni pasta, uncooked
1 lb. ground beef or ground Italian pork sausage
26-oz. jar pasta sauce, divided

1 c. shredded Monterey Jack cheese
1 c. shredded Cheddar cheese
Garnish: grated Parmesan cheese

Cook pasta according to package directions; drain. Meanwhile, brown meat in a skillet over medium heat; drain. Add pasta sauce, reserving 1/2 cup sauce. Simmer for 10 minutes. Spread reserved sauce in a 13"x9" baking pan coated with non-stick vegetable spray. Layer with half each of pasta, meat sauce and shredded cheeses; repeat layers. Sprinkle Parmesan cheese over top. Bake, uncovered, at 350 degrees for 30 minutes, or until hot and bubbly. Serves 4 to 6.

Italian Baked Chicken

Linda Rich
Bean Station, TN

When my kids were growing up, I had them make the evening meal once a week so they could learn to cook and plan. This chicken was my daughter's favorite dish...we always knew what to expect for supper on her night! She is now married with a family and is quite an accomplished cook. We still enjoy this dish often.

4 boneless, skinless chicken
    breasts
salt and pepper to taste
1/2 c. fat-free or regular Italian
    salad dressing

1/2 c. margarine, sliced
1/4 c. lemon juice
1/4 c. Worcestershire sauce
2 t. garlic powder or granulated
    garlic

Place chicken in a lightly greased 13"x9" baking pan. Season with salt and pepper; set aside. Combine remaining ingredients in a saucepan; cook over low heat until margarine melts. Drizzle over chicken. Bake, uncovered, at 325 degrees for 45 minutes, or until golden and chicken juices run clear when pierced. Serves 4.

Saucy Beans & Rice Italia

Sharon Crider
Junction City, KS

A tasty side dish that's ready to serve in minutes.

14-1/2 oz. can Italian-style
    diced tomatoes
2/3 c. instant rice, uncooked

1/4 t. Italian seasoning
15-1/2 oz. can cannellini beans,
    drained and rinsed

Combine undrained tomatoes and remaining ingredients in a saucepan over medium-high heat. Cover; cook 3 to 4 minutes. Uncover; cook an additional 2 to 3 minutes, or until slightly saucy and rice is tender. Serves 6.

Over dinner, ask your children to tell you about books they're reading at school and return the favor by sharing books you loved as a child. You may find you have some favorites in common!

Ravioli & Broccoletti

JoAnn
Gooseberry Patch

Frozen ravioli is a terrific dinnertime shortcut! It's delicious with broccoletti, a cross between broccoli and Chinese kale. We enjoy this meatless main with short cuts of asparagus too.

25-oz. pkg. frozen cheese
   ravioli, uncooked
1/4 to 1/2 c. butter
2 T. olive oil
3 cloves garlic, thinly sliced
2 lbs. broccoletti, trimmed and
   stems removed

1/4 t. salt
1/4 t. red pepper flakes
1 t. lemon zest
Garnish: grated Parmesan
   cheese

Cook ravioli according to package instructions. Drain, reserving one cup of cooking water. Meanwhile, melt butter with olive oil in a large skillet over medium-high heat. Add garlic and sauté until golden, about 3 minutes. Add broccoletti, seasonings and reserved cooking water to skillet; bring to a boil. Cover and cook about 5 minutes, stirring occasionally. Reduce heat; cook another 5 minutes, or until liquid evaporates and broccoletti is tender. Stir in lemon zest. Add ravioli to skillet; stir gently to coat well with butter mixture. Sprinkle with Parmesan cheese before serving. Serves 4 to 6.

Grow a pizza garden! Create a round garden sectioned into wedges. Plant basil, oregano, parsley and other fragrant herbs...add some tomatoes, peppers or other favorite pizza toppings. A terrific way to get kids interested in fresh foods!

Pasta e Fagioli Deliziosa

Erin Kolp
Litchfield, MN

My husband and two kids request this yummy soup of pasta and beans all the time. I'm happy to oblige since it's easy to fix and makes the house smell great. Serve with crusty French bread.

2 T. olive oil
1 c. onion, diced
3 cloves garlic, minced
2 14-1/2 oz. cans diced
   tomatoes
16-oz. can Great Northern beans

3 c. chicken broth
1/4 c. fresh Italian parsley,
   chopped
1 t. dried basil
1/4 t. pepper
2 c. small shell pasta, uncooked

Heat oil in a 4-quart Dutch oven over medium heat until hot; add onion. Cook and stir for 5 minutes, or until onion is tender. Add garlic; cook and stir for one minute. Add undrained tomatoes, undrained beans, broth, herbs and pepper. Bring to a boil over high heat, stirring occasionally. Reduce heat to low. Cover and simmer for 10 minutes without stirring. Add uncooked pasta. Cover and simmer for 12 to 15 minutes, just until pasta is tender. Serve immediately. Makes 8 servings.

Hang up an old-fashioned mini washboard where family messages, calendars and to-do lists can be easily found. Button magnets and clothespin clips will hold everything in place and add a dash of fun.

Bubbly Cheese Garlic Bread

Angie Bowan
Tarpon Springs, FL

My children love this delicious bread! All ingredients can be adjusted to your taste...use a mixture of all three cheeses, if you like.

1/2 c. butter, softened
1 to 2 cloves garlic, crushed
1/2 to 1 c. creamy Italian salad
   dressing
1 loaf Italian bread, halved
   lengthwise

2 c. shredded Cheddar,
   mozzarella or Monterey Jack
   cheese
2 t. dried parsley

Blend butter, garlic and salad dressing together in a small bowl. Place bread on a baking sheet, cut-side up. Spread butter mixture over both halves. Top with shredded cheese and parsley. Bake, uncovered, at 375 degrees for 10 to 20 minutes, until cheese is melted and bubbly. Slice each half into 8 pieces; serve warm. Makes 16 servings.

A whimsical centerpiece for an Italian dinner! Take a handful of long pasta like spaghetti, bucatini or curly strands of fusilli, and fan it out in a wide-mouthed vase.

Pasta Puttanesca

Brandi Joiner
Minot, ND

Such a versatile recipe! It's good either warm or cold...perfect for a potluck or a picnic. Stir in some sliced pepperoni, if you like.

16-oz. pkg. rotini pasta, uncooked
1 red onion, chopped
1 T. olive oil
5-oz. jar sliced green olives with pimentos, drained

4-oz. can sliced black olives, drained
24-oz. jar marinara sauce
Garnish: grated Parmesan cheese

Cook pasta according to package directions; drain. Meanwhile, in a large skillet over medium heat, sauté onion in olive oil until soft. Add olives; continue to sauté for another 2 to 3 minutes. Add pasta to the skillet and toss to mix. Add marinara sauce; stir well and heat through. Garnish with Parmesan cheese. Serves 6.

Green Bean Sauté

Emily Martin
Ontario, Canada

A simple side dish that comes together in a jiffy.

1/2 onion, cut into thin wedges
1 clove garlic, minced
1/2 t. dried basil
1 T. olive oil

2 14-1/2 oz. cans green beans, drained
14-1/2 oz. can petite diced tomatoes, drained

In a saucepan over medium heat, combine onion, garlic, basil and oil. Sauté for about 5 minutes, until onion is tender. Add green beans and tomatoes; heat through. Makes 4 to 6 servings.

Add flavor to pasta...drop a cube or two of chicken or beef bouillon into the cooking water along with the pasta. It works with rice too!

Wednesday is Italian Night

Dawn's Penne Siciliano

Dawn Raskiewicz
Alliance, NE

My husband spent a year stationed in Sicily while in the Air Force. He loves Italian food, so I created this one-pot recipe for him. It was a hit! Add homemade garlic bread to complete the meal.

1/2 lb. lean ground beef
1/4 green pepper, diced
1/2 onion, diced
1 to 2 t. garlic, minced
garlic salt and pepper to taste
32-oz. jar pasta sauce
1-3/4 to 2 c. water

7-oz. can mushroom stems and
   pieces, drained
8-oz. pkg. penne rigate pasta,
   uncooked
Garnish: grated Parmesan
   cheese or shredded Italian-
   blend cheese

In a large skillet over medium heat, cook beef, green pepper and onion. Stir in garlic when beef is almost done. Continue cooking until beef is well browned; drain. Add seasonings, pasta sauce, water and mushrooms; stir to blend. Mix in uncooked pasta. Cover and simmer, stirring occasionally, until pasta is tender, about 10 minutes. Top with cheese. Serves 4 to 6.

Watch for old-fashioned clear glass canisters at tag sales and flea markets...perfect countertop storage for all kinds of pasta.

Chicago Italian Beef

Heather Porter
Villa Park, IL

*If you come from Chicago you know Italian beef! Serve with chewy,
delicious Italian rolls and top with some of the gravy from
the slow cooker...the taste is out of this world!*

4 to 5-lb. beef rump roast or
   bottom round roast
16-oz. jar pepperoncini
16-oz. jar mild giardiniera mix
   in oil

14-oz. can beef broth
1.05-oz. pkg. Italian salad
   dressing mix
8 to 16 Italian rolls, split

Place roast in a large slow cooker. Top with undrained pepperoncini
and giardeniera; pour in broth and sprinkle with dressing mix. Cover
and cook on low setting for 6 to 8 hours. Reserving liquid in slow
cooker, shred beef with 2 forks. To serve, top rolls with beef and some
of the liquid and vegetables from slow cooker. Serves 8 to 16.

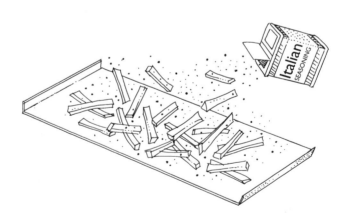

Spice up some frozen French fries to serve with shredded beef
sandwiches! Simply spritz the fries with olive oil, then sprinkle with
Italian seasoning and garlic powder before popping them in the
oven. Bake as the package directs, tossing several times,
until crisp and golden.

Simple Stromboli

Diane Williams
Mountain Top, PA

*I love this recipe because you can mix & match deli meats
and cheeses to suit everyone's taste.*

1 green pepper, thinly sliced
1 onion, thinly sliced
1 T. butter
13.8-oz. tube refrigerated pizza
   crust

1/2 lb. deli ham or roast beef,
   thinly sliced
8 slices mozzarella cheese
pepper to taste

In a skillet over medium heat, sauté green pepper and onion in butter until tender. Unroll unbaked pizza crust on a lightly greased baking sheet. Layer crust with slices of meat and cheese; top with green pepper mixture and season with pepper. Roll crust loosely into a tube, jelly-roll style; pinch top and sides closed. Bake, seam-side down, at 375 degrees for about 25 minutes, until golden. Slice to serve. Serves 4.

Tuck a tiny Italian flag toothpick in your sandwiches! Not only fun, they're great for holding together overstuffed sandwiches.

Linguine & Clams

Elizabeth Cisneros
Eastvale, CA

A classic Italian restaurant favorite to savor at home.

16-oz. pkg. linguine pasta,
   uncooked
1/4 c. butter
1/4 c. olive oil
4 cloves garlic, minced

1 c. white wine or clam broth
10-oz. can whole baby clams,
   drained and liquid reserved
2 T. fresh parsley, minced
Garnish: cracked pepper

Cook pasta according to package directions, just until tender; drain. Meanwhile, melt butter with olive oil in a large skillet over medium heat. Add garlic; sauté until tender. Stir in wine or broth and reserved clam liquid; simmer for 10 minutes. Stir in clams and parsley; simmer for 5 more minutes. Toss pasta with sauce; garnish with a sprinkle of pepper. Serves 4.

Homemade Fettuccine Alfredo

Denise Webb
Savannah, GA

Oh how I love fettuccine alfredo! I like to make it extra delicious by adding some sautéed garlic and spinach, sometimes even shrimp or scallops. Yum!

8-oz. pkg. fettuccine or linguine
   pasta, uncooked
7 T. butter, softened

1 c. half-and-half
1 to 1-1/2 c. grated Parmesan
   cheese

Cook pasta according to package directions, just until tender; drain and return to cooking pot. Add butter and half-and-half; stir until butter melts and mixture is heated through. Add Parmesan cheese; stir until thickened. Makes 4 to 6 servings.

Friendships and macaroni are best when they are warm.

– Old Italian saying

Mama's Bisghetti

Jennifer Rubino
Hickory, NC

I'm Italian by marriage only, but I've made my mark by perfecting this slow-cooker sauce. Now this is everyone's favorite birthday supper, including my son David, who thought spaghetti started with a B! Mix it up by using two different flavors of pasta sauce.

1 lb. ground pork sausage
1 lb. lean ground beef
1 onion, diced
1 green pepper, diced
8-oz. jar sliced mushrooms, drained
2 26-oz. jars pasta sauce

Optional: 1 c. red wine
16-oz. pkg. angel hair pasta, cooked
Garnish: grated Parmesan cheese, crumbled feta cheese
Optional: toasted pine nuts

Brown sausage in a large skillet over medium heat. Drain on paper towels; set aside. In the same skillet, brown beef with onion, green pepper and mushrooms; drain. In a large slow cooker, combine sauce, sausage, beef mixture and wine, if using; stir. Cover and cook on low setting for 4 hours. Serve sauce over cooked pasta; garnish with cheeses and pine nuts, if desired. Serves 6.

Make a warm loaf of crostini for dinner...a tasty go-with for pasta.
Slice a loaf of Italian bread into 1/2-inch slices. Brush olive oil
over both sides of each slice; sprinkle with coarse salt. Bake in a
300-degree oven for 20 minutes, or until toasty, turning once.

Italian Roast with Polenta

Krystal Sowell
Spring, TX

A terrific recipe for company...it looks like it took hours to prepare!
Only you know you have the slow cooker to thank.

8-oz. can tomato sauce
1-1/4 oz. pkg. pasta sauce mix,
  divided
3-lb. beef tri-tip roast or flank
  steak

2 t. olive oil
1/2 onion, chopped
3 carrots, peeled and chopped
14-1/2 oz. can Italian-style
  diced tomatoes

In a large slow cooker, stir together tomato sauce and half of sauce mix; set aside. Rub roast with remaining sauce mix. Heat olive oil in a large skillet over medium-high heat; brown roast on all sides. Remove roast to a large slow cooker. Add onion and carrots to the same skillet; cook until soft. Remove skillet from heat; stir in tomatoes. Pour onion mixture over roast in slow cooker. Cover and cook on low setting for 8 hours, or until roast is tender. To serve, divide Parmesan Polenta among dinner plates. Top with slices of roast and a generous spoonful of sauce. Serves 6 to 8.

Parmesan Polenta:

4 c. reduced-sodium chicken
  broth

1 c. yellow cornmeal
1/2 c. grated Parmesan cheese

In a saucepan over medium-high heat, bring broth to a boil. Add cornmeal; cook until thickened, stirring frequently. Reduce heat to low. Stir in cheese; cover and cook for 5 minutes.

For just a hint of garlic flavor, slice a garlic clove in half and rub the insides of individual wooden salad bowls.

Italian Tomato Salad

Linda Rich
Bean Station, TN

My husband has a special knack for putting this salad together using our delicious locally grown tomatoes. We serve it with steak, chicken and everything Italian. Dip some crusty Italian bread in the dressing for a real treat!

2 to 3 tomatoes, cut into bite-size pieces
1 T. fresh basil, chopped, or 1 t. dried basil

1 T. olive oil
1 T. red wine vinegar
1 c. fat-free Italian salad dressing

In a salad bowl, mix all ingredients together. Cover and chill for at least 30 minutes. Toss again just before serving. Makes 4 servings.

Polenta is a terrific side dish for saucy Italian dishes. Topped with marinara sauce and sautéed mushrooms, it can even serve as a meatless main dish. You can find ready-to-use polenta in the supermarket's refrigerated section... easy to slice, heat and serve.

Yummy Chicken Italiano

Karyn Born
Coconut Creek, FL

This slow-cooker recipe is one of my family's favorite dinners, and no one realizes it is low in fat! Even my two kids, aged two and five, love it. When company is coming, I like to make a double batch to serve with a salad and bread sticks...always a crowd-pleaser!

1 to 2 lbs. boneless, skinless chicken breasts, cut into 1-inch cubes
1/4 c. water
.7-oz. pkg. Italian salad dressing mix
1/2 c. onion, chopped
1 clove garlic, chopped
10-3/4 oz. can fat-free cream of chicken soup
1/2 c. chicken broth
8-oz. pkg. reduced-fat cream cheese, cubed
16-oz. pkg. rotini pasta or wide egg noodles, cooked

Place chicken in a slow cooker; sprinkle with water and salad dressing mix. Cover and cook on low setting for 4 hours. Spray a large saucepan with non-stick vegetable spray; sauté onion and garlic for one to 2 minutes. Add soup, broth and cream cheese to saucepan. Stir until cream cheese is melted and mixture is smooth. Add soup mixture to slow cooker; cover and cook on low setting for one additional hour. Add cooked pasta or noodles to slow cooker just before serving; mix thoroughly. Serves 6.

If dinner isn't quite ready and tummies are rumbling, set out a simple antipasto platter of fresh veggies, ripe olives and cubes of mozzarella cheese for nibbling.

Wednesday is Italian Night

Creamy Tomato Tortellini

April Burdette
Parkersburg, WV

When I serve this meatless main dish, there are never any leftovers!
It's easy to make and tastes great. My 16-year-old daughter
is a very picky eater, and she loves this dish.

9-oz. pkg. frozen cheese
  tortellini, uncooked
2 c. broccoli flowerets
14-1/2 oz. can Italian-style
  diced tomatoes

8-oz. pkg. cream cheese, cubed
1 t. Italian seasoning
Garnish: grated Parmesan
  cheese

Cook tortellini according to package directions; add broccoli to cooking water for last 3 minutes of cooking time. Drain. Meanwhile, in a skillet over medium heat, simmer undrained tomatoes for 5 minutes. Stir in cream cheese and seasoning. Cook, stirring often, for 2 to 3 minutes, until cream cheese is melted and mixture is well blended. Add tortellini mixture to tomato mixture; toss lightly. Sprinkle with Parmesan cheese. Serves 4 to 6.

Tina's Savory Bruschetta

Tina Muldoon
Sparta, NJ

We've been making this bruschetta for years...it's easy
and always a hit!

.7-oz. pkg. Italian salad dressing
  mix
4 tomatoes, diced

1/2 c. red onion, minced
salt and pepper to taste
1 loaf Italian bread, thinly sliced

In a bowl, prepare dressing mix according to instructions. Add tomatoes and onion to dressing; season with salt and pepper. Cover and refrigerate for 2 hours to overnight. At serving time, place bread slices on an ungreased baking sheet. Bake at 350 degrees until lightly toasted, 5 to 10 minutes. Top bread slices with dollops of tomato mixture. Makes about 10 servings.

Becki's Baked Spaghetti

Becki Blanchard
Clifton, ID

My five kids and husband, who are all choosy eaters, love my baked spaghetti! It's simple, delicious and easy on our budget.

16-oz. pkg. spaghetti, uncooked
2 lbs. ground Italian pork
   sausage
1 onion, chopped
10-3/4 oz. can cream of
   mushroom soup

8-oz. can tomato sauce
1 c. plus 2 T. water
1 c. grated Parmesan cheese
seasoned salt, garlic pepper and
   Italian seasoning to taste
2 c. shredded Cheddar cheese

Cook spaghetti according to package directions; drain. Meanwhile, brown sausage and onion in a large skillet over medium-high heat; drain. Add remaining ingredients except Cheddar cheese to skillet. Reduce heat to low; simmer for 10 minutes. Place cooked spaghetti in a greased deep 13"x9" baking pan. Add sausage mixture to spaghetti; mix gently. Sprinkle Cheddar cheese on top. Cover and bake at 350 degrees for 25 minutes, or until hot and bubbly. Makes 10 servings.

For baked pasta casseroles, cook pasta for the shortest cooking time recommended on the package. It's not necessary to rinse the cooked pasta; just drain well.

One-Pot Saucy Rotini

Brandi Hilfiker
Holtville, CA

As a mom of four, I know I can count on this dish...it has a little bit of everything my kids love. They always want seconds! Best of all, it's ready to serve in 30 minutes or less.

14-oz. smoked beef or turkey
    sausage link, sliced
1 onion, chopped
3-1/2 c. water

26-oz. jar pasta sauce
3 c. rotini pasta, uncooked
1 c. sliced mushrooms
1 c. shredded mozzarella cheese

In a deep skillet over medium heat, brown sausage and onion; drain. Add water, sauce and uncooked pasta; cover. Bring to a boil. Reduce heat to low. Simmer, uncovered, for 20 minutes, stirring occasionally, until pasta is tender. Add mushrooms; cook 5 minutes. Stir in cheese. Serves 6.

Try cavatappi pasta or extra-long fusilli pasta in a favorite recipe. With extra twists and turns, these corkscrew-shaped pastas hold the sauce very well...and are just plain fun to eat!

Marvelous Minestrone

Barbara Bowen
Lewiston, ID

This hearty veggie-filled soup takes awhile to simmer, but it's so simple to toss together that you won't mind at all. It freezes well, so why not make a double batch?

1/4 c. olive oil
2 cloves garlic, chopped
1 c. onion, chopped
5 stalks celery, chopped
6 c. beef broth
2 6-oz. cans tomato paste
2 carrots, peeled and diced
2 leeks, chopped

2 c. cabbage, chopped
2 to 3 potatoes, peeled and diced
1 t. dried rosemary
salt and pepper to taste
15-1/2 oz. can kidney beans
3/4 c. elbow macaroni, uncooked
Garnish: grated Parmesan
 cheese

Heat oil in a large pot over medium heat; sauté garlic, onion and celery until tender. Stir in remaining ingredients except beans, macaroni and garnish. Bring to a boil; reduce heat to low. Cover and simmer for one hour, stirring occasionally. Stir in undrained beans and uncooked macaroni. Simmer, uncovered, for another 30 minutes, stirring occasionally, until macaroni is tender. Serve sprinkled with Parmesan cheese. Makes 8 to 10 servings.

Stock your freezer with comforting home-cooked soups and sauces, ready to enjoy anytime! They freeze well for up to three months in plastic freezer containers. To serve, thaw overnight in the refrigerator. Thin with a little water when reheating, if needed.

Joe's Italian Steak Sandwiches

Augusta Gillard
Essexville, MI

When I married my husband 20 years ago, he showed me how to make his delicious steak sandwiches. They're still a favorite!

4 ground beef sirloin patties
4-oz. can sliced mushrooms, drained
26-oz. can pasta sauce with garlic & herbs

8 slices Italian bread, sliced 1/2-inch thick on the diagonal
1/4 c. butter, softened
4 to 8 slices Muenster cheese

In a skillet over medium-high heat, cook beef patties with mushrooms until patties are browned and cooked through. Meanwhile, warm pasta sauce in a saucepan over low heat. Spread one side of each bread slice with butter. On a griddle over medium-high heat, grill bread slices butter-side down until golden. For each sandwich, place one bread slice on a sandwich plate, grilled-side down. Top with a generous scoop of sauce, a beef patty, some mushrooms, more sauce and one to 2 cheese slices. Add another bread slice, grilled-side up, and slice to serve. Makes 4 sandwiches.

Sandwiches are a tasty mealtime solution when family members will be dining at different times. Fix sandwiches ahead of time, wrap individually in aluminum foil and refrigerate. Pop them into a toaster oven or under a broiler to heat...fresh, full of flavor and ready whenever you are!

Gina's Mangia Meatballs

Gina O'Connor
Lake Villa, IL

I really enjoy spending time in the kitchen with my four children...and they love it when I make meatballs! They like to help mix all the ingredients and shape them. Leftover meatballs are perfect for sub sandwiches later in the week, so this is a cook-once, eat-twice kind of meal. What busy mom doesn't like that?

3/4 lb. lean ground beef	2 T. garlic, minced
3/4 lb. lean ground pork	2 t. dried parsley
1/2 c. soft bread crumbs	1 t. dried oregano
1/4 c. grated Parmesan cheese	1 t. sea salt
1 egg, lightly beaten	1 t. pepper
1/2 c. milk	

Mix all ingredients together in a large bowl. If mixture seems too wet, add more bread crumbs. Form mixture lightly into meatballs, using about 2 tablespoons of mixture for each one. Place meatballs on an ungreased rimmed baking sheet. Bake, uncovered, at 350 degrees for about 30 minutes, until no longer pink in the center. Meatballs may also be added to pasta sauce and simmered on the stovetop until cooked through, about 45 minutes. Serves 6 to 8.

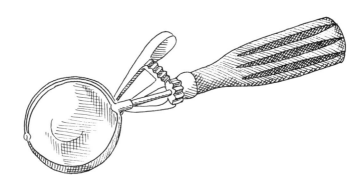

Making lots of meatballs? Grab a mini ice cream scoop or melon baller and start scooping...you'll be done in record time!

Wednesday is **Italian Night**

Grandma's Spaghetti Sauce

April Davidson
Lily, KY

My favorite childhood memories are of family dinners at my grandma's house. Whenever she made her spaghetti sauce she would let me add the seasonings, which led to my love for cooking. Her spaghetti sauce was definitely a favorite...I fix it often now using my own blend of seasonings.

1 lb. ground beef chuck
3 14-1/2 oz. cans stewed
   tomatoes
6-oz. can tomato paste
1/4 c. diced onion
1 clove garlic, minced

1 t. Italian seasoning
1/2 t. garlic salt
1/2 t. onion salt
1 bay leaf
salt and pepper to taste
3 semi-sweet chocolate chips

Place beef in a large pot; break up with a spatula. Add enough water to cover beef; bring to a boil over medium-high heat. Cook until beef is no longer pink; drain and return beef to pot. Pour undrained tomatoes into a blender; process to a liquid consistency. Add tomatoes to pot; stir in remaining ingredients except chocolate chips. Reduce heat to low and simmer for 30 minutes. Discard bay leaf; stir in chocolate chips. Simmer for another 10 minutes. Makes 6 servings.

Wondering how much spaghetti to cook for dinner? A single, one-cup portion of cooked spaghetti equals a 1/2-inch bundle of uncooked spaghetti strands. You'll get eight servings from a one-pound package.

Beth's Cavatini

Melissa Knight
Athens, AL

This quick & easy recipe was given to me by my dear friend Beth.
We are both newly married and love to trade fun and
thrifty recipes like this one.

16-oz. pkg. rigatoni pasta,
   uncooked
1 lb. ground pork sausage
1 onion, diced

1 green pepper, diced
26-oz. jar pasta sauce
3-1/2 oz. pkg. sliced pepperoni
2 c. shredded mozzarella cheese

Cook pasta according to package directions; drain. Meanwhile, brown
sausage in a skillet over medium heat. Add onion and green pepper;
cook until tender. Drain; stir in pasta sauce. Combine pasta and
sausage mixture; mix together and transfer to a greased 13"x9" baking
pan. Arrange pepperoni slices on top; sprinkle with cheese. Bake,
uncovered, at 350 degrees for 20 minutes, or until hot and bubbly.
Serves 6 to 8.

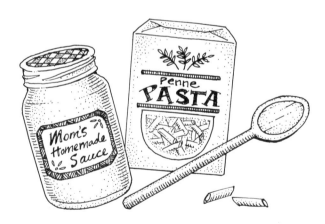

There are lots of delicious, already-seasoned flavors of pasta sauce
at the supermarket! Keep several different varieties in the pantry
and add a new twist to tried & true dishes.

Simple 2-Cheese Lasagna

Kathy Grashoff
Fort Wayne, IN

When I had my parents over for dinner, my dad must have told me four times how good this lasagna was! It's an easy make-ahead too.

1 lb. ground mild Italian pork
  sausage
2 32-oz. jars pasta sauce,
  divided
8 no-boil lasagna noodles,
  uncooked

16-oz. container ricotta cheese,
  divided
16-oz. pkg. shredded mozzarella
  cheese, divided

Brown sausage in a skillet over medium heat; drain well. Spread one cup pasta sauce in a greased 13"x9" baking pan; layer with 4 noodles crosswise. In a bowl, combine remaining sauce and sausage; spread half of mixture over noodles. Dollop with half the ricotta cheese; sprinkle with half the mozzarella cheese. Repeat layers, ending with mozzarella cheese. Bake, uncovered, at 350 degrees for 30 minutes, or until hot and bubbly. Makes 8 servings.

Herbed Parmesan Squash

Jenn Vallimont
Kersey, PA

My mom serves this recipe often for special occasions. It's a terrific recipe for summertime when squash is plentiful.

1/4 c. butter
2 zucchini, diced
2 yellow squash, diced
1 onion, diced
1 t. dried oregano

1/4 t. garlic powder
1/4 t. salt
1/2 t. pepper
1/2 c. grated Parmesan cheese

Melt butter in a skillet over medium heat. Add vegetables; sauté for 10 minutes. Stir in seasonings. Cover and cook over low heat an additional 10 minutes, or to desired tenderness. Sprinkle with Parmesan cheese; cover and simmer over very low heat for 5 minutes. Serves 4 to 6.

Easy Batter-Crust Pizza

Amber Beckman
Anna, OH

This homemade pizza is oh-so good...and you won't even need yeast or a box mix to make it!

1-1/2 lbs. ground beef or ground pork sausage
1 c. plus 2 T. all-purpose flour, divided
1 t. Italian seasoning
1/2 t. salt
1-1/2 t. pepper
2/3 c. milk
2 eggs, beaten
1/4 c. onion, chopped
Optional: 4-oz. can sliced mushrooms, drained
8-oz. can pizza sauce
1 c. shredded mozzarella cheese

In a skillet over medium heat, brown beef or sausage; drain well. Meanwhile, lightly grease a 12" round pizza pan; sprinkle with 2 tablespoons flour and set aside. In a small bowl, combine remaining flour, seasonings, milk and eggs; whisk until smooth. Pour batter into pizza pan, tilting pan so batter covers the bottom. Spoon beef or sausage over batter; top with onion and mushrooms, if using. Bake on the lowest oven rack at 425 degrees for 25 to 30 minutes, until deeply golden. Spread pizza sauce over pizza; top with cheese. Bake for an additional 10 to 15 minutes. Cut into wedges to serve. Makes 6 servings.

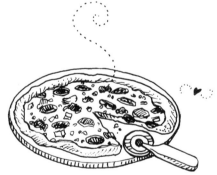

Homemade pizza is super for easy, thrifty family meals. Top an oven-ready crust with pizza sauce, then check the fridge for leftover cooked veggies and meat. Add toppings and cheese as you like, then pop it into a 400-degree oven until heated through and the cheese is melted. Yum!

Pesto Chicken Pizza

Connie Ramsey
Pontotoc, MS

This is my kids' favorite pizza, and their friends love it too. Cut into small squares, it makes a great appetizer. Feel free to add the chicken, or not...we like the pizza just as well without it!

12-inch unbaked pizza crust
8-oz. jar pesto sauce
1 c. grilled chicken, chopped

1 c. shredded Italian-blend
    cheese
1 c. Gouda cheese, shredded

Place crust on an ungreased baking sheet; prebake, if specified by package directions. Spread desired amount of pesto sauce over crust. Sprinkle chicken over pesto; top with cheeses. Bake at 400 degrees for about 10 minutes, until crust is golden and cheese is bubbly. Makes 4 to 6 servings.

You may be able to purchase fresh, unbaked pizza dough from your favorite pizza shop. It's also often found in the refrigerator case at the supermarket.

Slow-Cooked Spaghetti & Pork

Glenda Barrick
Roosevelt, AZ

When John & I were first married, he told me that spaghetti was the only dish he wouldn't eat. I really like it, so after awhile, I decided to fix it anyway. I asked him to give it a try, and if he didn't like it, I would make him something else. He took one bite and told me I could make spaghetti for him anytime! This delicious recipe is an easy way to feed a crowd. Just add garlic toast and a tossed salad.

4 lbs. country-style pork ribs,
    cut into serving-size pieces
garlic salt and pepper to taste
67-oz. jar pasta sauce
14-1/2 oz. can diced tomatoes
6-oz. can tomato paste
1 c. Lambrusco or Zinfandel
    wine or water
1 onion, chopped
1/4 c. grated Parmesan cheese

1 T. garlic, minced, or more to
    taste
1 t. Italian seasoning
1/2 t. sugar
1 to 2 16-oz. pkgs. spaghetti,
    cooked
Garnish: additional grated
    Parmesan cheese,
    red pepper flakes

Season ribs with garlic salt and pepper; arrange in a large slow cooker. Add remaining ingredients except spaghetti and garnish; stir together. Cover and cook on low setting for 8 hours, or until ribs are very tender. Remove ribs from sauce; arrange on a serving platter. To serve, either place cooked spaghetti on dinner plates and top with sauce, or add sauce to the drained spaghetti in its pot, toss to mix and transfer to a serving bowl. Garnish with additional Parmesan cheese and red pepper flakes. Serves 8 to 10.

Quick and clever napkin rings! When serving pasta for dinner, slip napkins through an uncooked manicotti tube.

Wednesday is Italian Night

Tomato Bread Salad

Patricia Flak
Erie, PA

*Easy, easy, easy...and can be made at the last minute
when unexpected company arrives!*

6 slices day-old rustic Italian
   bread, crusts removed
1/4 to 1/2 c. water
2 tomatoes, chopped
1/4 cucumber, thinly sliced
1 bunch green onions, thinly
   sliced

25 leaves fresh basil, torn
3 T. fresh parsley, chopped
5 T. olive oil
3 T. red wine vinegar
salt and pepper to taste

Tear or slice bread into 3/4-inch pieces; place in a large salad bowl.
Sprinkle bread with water until moistened but not soggy. Add
remaining ingredients; toss to mix well. Serve immediately. Makes
6 servings.

Parmesan Pull-Aparts

Barbara Sturm
Bakersfield, CA

*Recruit your kids to roll the dough balls. They'll have fun
both making and eating these yummy rolls.*

3 T. butter
1 t. sesame seed
1/2 t. celery seed
1 T. dried, minced onion

10-oz. tube refrigerated flaky
   biscuits, quartered
1/4 c. grated Parmesan cheese

In a 400-degree oven, melt butter in a 9" round cake pan. Remove pan
from oven; sprinkle seeds and onion evenly over butter. Meanwhile,
roll biscuit pieces into balls; place in a large plastic zipping bag. Add
cheese; shake to coat. Arrange dough balls evenly in pan. Sprinkle
with any remaining cheese from bag. Bake at 400 degrees for 15 to
18 minutes, until golden. Makes 10 servings.

Heavenly Lasagna Soup

Bethi Hendrickson
Danville, PA

This is a stick-to-your-ribs kind of soup, wonderful on a cold winter day. My family calls it "a little taste of heaven in a bowl." It doesn't take long to prepare...you don't even precook the pasta.

1 lb. ground beef
3 cloves garlic, minced
8 c. chicken broth
26-oz. jar pasta sauce
2 14-1/2 oz. cans stewed
    tomatoes, broken up
6-oz. can tomato paste
2 T. Italian seasoning

1 c. ricotta cheese
2 c. shredded Italian-blend
    cheese
16-oz. pkg. campanelle pasta,
    uncooked
Garnish: grated Parmesan
    cheese

In a skillet over medium heat, brown beef with garlic. Drain and set aside. In a large stockpot, combine chicken broth, pasta sauce, undrained tomatoes, tomato paste and beef mixture; bring to a boil. Reduce heat to low. Add seasoning and cheeses; stir constantly until cheeses are melted completely. Add uncooked pasta to pot and cook about 20 minutes, stirring frequently, until pasta is tender. Remove from heat; let stand for 5 minutes. Serve in deep bowls; top with Parmesan cheese. Makes 10 to 12 servings.

What kind of olive oil to use? Less-expensive "light" olive oil is fine for cooking purposes. Reserve extra-virgin olive oil for delicately flavored salad dressings and dipping sauces.

Farmhouse Quiche, page 40

Chile Relleno Casserole, page 35

Mom's Macaroni & Cheese, page 13

Kristy's Zucchini Sticks, page 210

Caprese Salad, page 98

Mushroom-Barley Soup, page 19

Dad's Wimpy Burgers, page 206

Sesame-Asparagus Salad, page 33

Lemon Wine Chicken Skillet, page 151

Meatball-Stuffed Shells, page 99

Crispy Corn Fritters, page 35

Mexican Chicken Chili,
page 69

Just-for-Fun Fruit Pizza,
page 217

Cheddar Baked Spaghetti, page 38

Simple Stromboli, page 107

Chinese Chicken Wings, page 198

Chicago Italian Beef,
page 106

Mexicali Chicken Stack-Ups, page 48

Pineapple-Cherry Cake, page 176

Lil's Fiesta Cornbread, page 71

Tuna Noodle Casserole, page 155

Simple Baked Mostaccioli, page 98

Warm 3-Cheese Bread

Michele Olson
Safety Harbor, FL

Scrumptious with your favorite soup!

1 loaf French bread, halved
   lengthwise
6-oz. pkg. sliced mozzarella
   cheese
6 T. butter, melted

1/2 c. grated Parmesan cheese
1/2 c. grated Romano cheese
1/4 t. garlic powder
1 T. dried parsley

Place bread on a baking sheet, cut-side up. Top with mozzarella cheese slices and set aside. Mix remaining ingredients in a bowl; spread mixture over cheese slices. Bake at 375 degrees for 10 to 15 minutes, until cheese is bubbly and edges of bread are toasty. Slice; serve warm. Makes 8 to 10 servings.

Parmesan Herb Sprinkle

Robin Hill
Rochester, NY

A flavorful all 'round seasoning for cooked pasta, garlic bread and tossed salads. Maybe you'll come up with other uses too!

8-oz. container grated Parmesan
   cheese
3 T. Italian seasoning

3 T. dried parsley
1 T. garlic powder
1/2 t. cayenne pepper

Mix all ingredients well; place in a covered shaker jar. Keep refrigerated. Makes 2 cups.

Cute-as-a-button kitchen magnets! Look through Grandma's button box to find a variety of buttons. Hot-glue each button to a small magnet, and it's ready to keep recipes and shopping lists handy on the fridge.

Rustic Pasta Florentine

Tracy Roskoski
Edison, NJ

One night I was looking for something different for dinner, and my husband suggested pasta. Being a pasta lover, I quickly agreed! So I created this dish, and now he requests it almost once a week. Feel free to substitute your favorite short pasta.

16-oz. pkg. mini bowtie pasta, uncooked
1 lb. ground sweet Italian pork sausage
2 T. butter, divided
2 cloves garlic, minced
10-oz. pkg. frozen chopped spinach, thawed

15-oz. can diced tomatoes with garlic and onion
4-oz. can sliced mushrooms, drained
garlic powder and pepper to taste
Garnish: grated Parmesan cheese

Cook pasta according to package directions; drain. Meanwhile, in a skillet over medium heat, cook sausage until no longer pink; remove to paper towels to drain. In the same skillet, melt one tablespoon butter; add garlic and sauté for one minute. Stir in remaining butter, spinach, undrained tomatoes, mushrooms and seasonings. Add sausage and reduce heat to medium-low; simmer while pasta finishes cooking. Add sauce to cooked pasta; toss to mix well. Garnish with Parmesan cheese. Makes 4 servings.

Wide-rimmed soup plates are perfect for serving saucy pasta dishes as well as hearty dinner portions of soup.

128

Spicy Bowties & Sausage

Jeanne Mason
Cypress, TX

This is a most-requested dish...it's as good as you'll find in a restaurant, yet super easy to make. A terrific dish to serve to guests, or for a special family dinner!

12-oz. pkg. bowtie pasta, uncooked
1 lb. ground sweet Italian pork sausage
1/2 t. red pepper flakes
1/2 c. onion, chopped
3 cloves garlic, minced

28-oz. can whole Italian tomatoes, drained and chopped
1 c. fat-free half-and-half
1/2 t. salt
Optional: chopped fresh parsley or rosemary

Cook pasta according to package directions, just until tender; drain. Meanwhile, in a deep skillet, brown sausage with red pepper flakes over medium heat; drain. Add onion and garlic; cook until tender. Stir in tomatoes, half-and-half and salt. Reduce heat to low and simmer until thickened, about 8 to 10 minutes. Stir in cooked pasta. Garnish with chopped parsley or rosemary, if desired. Makes 4 servings.

Store onions and garlic away from other produce, in a dark well-ventilated pantry...they can cause other vegetables to soften when stored together.

Sylvia's Chicken & Artichokes

Teri Lindquist
Gurnee, IL

Many years ago, my dear friend Sylvia gave me a version of this recipe. We loved it, and since I like to play with recipes, over the years I reworked it, adding the lemon and artichokes. Sylvia fought a valiant 13-year fight with breast cancer, and passed away five years ago. I think she would have really enjoyed this dish.

4 chicken breasts	1/4 c. dry white wine or water
.7-oz. pkg. Italian salad dressing mix	14-oz. can artichoke quarters, drained
1/3 c. lemon juice	1 lemon, thinly sliced
1/3 c. olive oil	

Place chicken in a large plastic zipping bag; set aside. In a small bowl, whisk together dressing mix, lemon juice, olive oil and wine or water; pour over chicken. Seal bag; refrigerate 4 hours to overnight, turning several times to coat. Place chicken in a lightly greased 13"x9" baking pan, reserving marinade. Arrange artichokes and lemon slices around chicken. Bring marinade to a full boil in a small saucepan; let cool, then drizzle over chicken. Bake, uncovered, at 350 degrees for 45 minutes to one hour, basting once or twice with pan juices, until chicken is golden and juices run clear. If boneless, skinless chicken breasts are used, reduce baking time to 35 to 40 minutes. Pour pan juices into a gravy boat; stir well and serve with chicken. Serves 4.

For a tasty change from butter, serve slices of warm Italian bread with dipping oil. Pour a thin layer of extra-virgin olive oil into saucers, drizzle with a little balsamic vinegar and sprinkle with dried oregano. Scrumptious!

Chicken Tetrazzini

Nancy Gasko
South Bend, IN

*I couldn't find a tetrazzini recipe that my family enjoyed,
so I combined several recipes until I came up with this one.
We love it...one pan for now, one for later!*

12-oz. pkg. spaghetti, uncooked
1/2 c. butter
1/2 c. all-purpose flour
1 t. salt
1/4 to 1/2 t. white pepper
2 c. chicken broth
12-oz. can evaporated milk
1 c. milk
Optional: 1/4 c. dry sherry
4 c. cooked chicken, cubed
2 4-oz. cans sliced mushrooms, drained
3/4 to 1 c. grated Parmesan-Romano cheese, divided

Cook spaghetti according to package directions; drain. Meanwhile, melt butter in a Dutch oven over medium heat. Stir in flour, salt and pepper until smooth; cook for one to 2 minutes. Add chicken broth, milks and sherry, if using; bring to a boil and stir until thickened. Stir in chicken, mushrooms and cooked spaghetti. Divide between 2 greased 11"x7" baking pans; sprinkle with cheese. Bake one pan, uncovered, at 350 degrees for 20 to 30 minutes, until hot and bubbly; serve. Remaining pan may be wrapped and kept frozen up to 3 months. To serve, thaw overnight in refrigerator. Bake, covered, at 350 degrees for 30 minutes. Uncover and bake another 15 to 20 minutes. Makes 2 pans; each serves 4.

Save extra cooked pasta for another meal. Place it in a plastic zipping bag, toss with a little olive oil to coat pasta, close tightly and refrigerate for 3 to 4 days. To reheat pasta, pour it into a metal colander and immerse colander in a pot of boiling water for one minute, then drain...ready to serve.

Crustless Ricotta Cheesecake

Phyllis Mayle
Hubbard, OH

This scrumptious dessert is one of our Italian favorites...it always makes me think of the friend who gave me the recipe years ago. Perfect for special occasions, yet so simple to make.

4 eggs, separated
2-1/2 c. ricotta cheese
12-oz. can evaporated milk
1 c. milk
1 c. sugar

1 t. salt
2 t. vanilla extract
21-oz. can cherry or blueberry
    pie filling

In a deep bowl, with an electric mixer on high speed, beat egg whites until stiff peaks form; set aside. In a separate large bowl, combine egg yolks and remaining ingredients except pie filling. Beat on medium speed until well blended; use a spoon to fold egg whites into yolk mixture. Pour into a 13"x9" baking pan coated with non-stick vegetable spray. Bake at 350 degrees for 45 minutes. Allow to cool completely; cover and chill before cutting into squares. At serving time, top with pie filling. Serves 8 to 10.

Stir up sweet memories...look through Mom's or Grandma's recipe box and rediscover a long-forgotten favorite dessert to share.

Strawberry Ice

Mia Rossi
Charlotte, NC

A light, refreshing make-ahead dessert...try other varieties of fresh fruit like pineapple too. Scoop into paper cups to serve.

3 c. strawberries, hulled
   and halved, or frozen
   strawberries, thawed
2 T. sugar

2 T. honey
1 T. lemon juice
3 c. crushed ice, divided

Combine strawberries, sugar, honey, lemon juice and 2 cups ice in a food processor or blender; process until chunky. Add remaining ice and blend until completely smooth. Pour mixture into a shallow baking pan; cover and freeze for 30 minutes. With a fork, scrape ice until slushy; cover and return to freezer until firm, about 2 hours. Makes 8 servings.

Elegant stemmed glasses are just right for serving up desserts like Strawberry Ice, ice cream and mousse...it's sure to make everyone feel extra special.

Chocolate Italian Love Cake

Shannon Re
Loudonville,

Being Italian, this is one of my favorite cakes. I like to make i
for Valentine's Day, Sweetest Day, anniversaries and
just anytime I want to show someone love!

18-1/4 oz. pkg. fudge marble
   cake mix
2 16-oz. containers ricotta
   cheese
4 eggs
1 c. sugar

1 t. vanilla extract
3.9-oz. pkg. instant chocolat
   pudding mix
1 c. milk
8-oz. container frozen whipp
   topping, thawed

Prepare cake mix according to package directions. Pour batters into
greased 13"x9" baking pan; swirl with a knife and set aside. Place
ricotta in a separate bowl. Add eggs, one at a time, beating after ea
addition. Stir in sugar and vanilla. Spoon ricotta mixture evenly ov
cake batter. Bake at 350 degrees for 70 minutes. Cool completely. I
separate bowl, beat together dry pudding mix and milk for 2 minut
fold in whipped topping. Spread over cooled cake. Cover and chill f
one to 2 hours before cutting into squares. Serves 10 to 12.

Savor iced dessert coffee after a hearty meal. Start with 4 cups
chilled coffee. Pour coffee into a blender with a scoop of vanill
ice cream and a dollop of chocolate syrup; process until smoot
Top mugs with whipped cream. Yum!

Butter-Baked Chicken

Ellen Folkman
Crystal Beach, FL

My husband loves this recipe. It's warm and comforting
on a cool fall or winter night. Mashed potatoes are
a must...the gravy is delicious!

1/4 c. butter, sliced
1 c. all-purpose flour
1 t. salt
1/2 t. pepper
12-oz. can evaporated milk,
  divided

4 chicken breasts
10-3/4 oz. can cream of chicken
  soup
1/4 c. water

Place butter in a 13"x9" baking pan; melt in a 350-degree oven and
set aside. Meanwhile, in a shallow bowl, combine flour, salt and
pepper. Add 1/2 cup evaporated milk to a separate shallow bowl. Dip
chicken pieces in milk; dredge in flour mixture. Arrange chicken,
skin-side up, in baking pan. Bake, uncovered, at 350 degrees for
35 minutes. In a small bowl, combine soup, water and remaining
milk. Turn chicken over; spoon soup mixture over chicken. Bake an
additional 35 minutes, or until chicken is no longer pink. Remove
chicken to a serving platter. Whisk gravy in pan until smooth. Spoon
gravy over chicken; serve any remaining gravy on the side. Serves 4.

If mashed potatoes are on the dinner menu, whip in a teaspoon
or so of baking powder, and they'll be extra light and fluffy.

Honey Chicken & Sweet Potatoes

Pamela Elkin
Asheville, NC

I recently went through my old recipe files and rediscovered this wonderful recipe. The honey mixture gives a delicious flavor to the chicken and sweet potatoes.

3 lbs. chicken
salt and pepper to taste
1/4 c. honey
1/4 c. Catalina French salad
   dressing

1/4 t. dried tarragon
16-oz. can sweet potatoes,
   drained

Sprinkle chicken pieces with salt and pepper; place skin-side down in a lightly greased 3-quart casserole dish. In a small bowl, mix honey, salad dressing and tarragon. Brush honey mixture lightly over chicken. Bake, uncovered, at 350 degrees for 30 minutes, brushing occasionally with honey mixture. Turn chicken over; brush again with honey mixture. Bake 10 minutes longer. Add sweet potatoes to dish. Bake 10 to 15 minutes longer, brushing chicken and potatoes occasionally with remaining honey mixture. Serve with pan juices. Makes 5 to 6 servings.

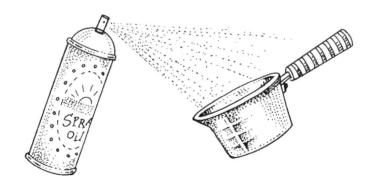

Spray a measuring cup with non-stick vegetable spray before measuring honey or peanut butter...the sticky stuff will slip right out.

Cheddar Meatloaf Roll-Ups

Andrea Heyart
Aubrey, TX

*My husband asks for this dish whenever he needs some
real comfort food. For the best flavor and texture,
chill overnight before baking.*

1-1/2 lbs. ground beef
1/2 c. dry bread crumbs, divided
3 T. barbecue sauce
1 egg, beaten
1/2 t. salt

1/4 t. pepper
1 c. shredded Cheddar cheese
1/4 c. green pepper
2 T. milk

In a large bowl, combine beef, 1/4 cup bread crumbs, barbecue sauce,
egg, salt and pepper. Mix well. On a long piece of aluminum foil, pat
beef mixture into a 13-inch by 8-inch rectangle. Combine remaining
bread crumbs and other ingredients; pat over beef mixture. Roll up beef
mixture jelly-roll style, starting on one long side; discard foil. Place in
an ungreased 13"x9" glass baking pan. Cover and chill overnight.
Uncover; bake at 350 degrees for 30 minutes. Slice to serve. Makes
6 servings.

Herbed Biscuits

Jennifer McIntosh
Pacific Palisades, CA

*I'm always asked to bring my Herbed Biscuits to get-togethers
and potlucks. They're so easy to make and hard to resist...no one
is satisfied with just one!*

1/2 c. butter, melted
1/4 t. dried thyme
1/8 t. paprika
1/8 t. poultry seasoning

1/8 t. salt
2 16.3-oz. tubes refrigerated
     buttermilk biscuits

In a shallow bowl, combine butter and seasonings; stir well. Dip
each biscuit into butter mixture, coating both sides; arrange in a
Bundt® pan. Bake at 350 degrees for 20 to 30 minutes, until golden,
checking after 20 minutes. Serves 8 to 10.

Scottish Shepherd's Pie

Vicki Shearer
Renton, WA

My Scottish husband loves this casserole...it smells so yummy baking on a cold winter's night. I like to use leftover mashed potatoes but, in a pinch, instant potatoes will do.

1 lb. lean ground beef	1-oz. pkg. brown gravy mix
1/2 c. yellow onion, diced	1 to 3 t. curry powder, to taste
1 c. carrot, peeled and diced	4 c. mashed potatoes, warmed

Brown beef, onion and carrot in a skillet over medium heat; drain. Meanwhile, prepare gravy mix according to package directions; stir desired amount of curry powder into gravy. Add gravy to beef mixture. Spoon into an ungreased 2-quart casserole dish. Top with warm mashed potatoes. Bake, uncovered, at 350 degrees for 30 to 35 minutes. Makes 4 to 6 servings.

Need an after-school snack for the kids? Head to the pantry and mix up crunchy cereal squares, mini pretzels, raisins and nuts...toss in a few candy-coated chocolates for fun!

Jan's Pork Chops & Pierogies

Janet Hall
Maple Heights, OH

When the weather turns chilly, there's nothing like having
a hot meal ready in the slow cooker when you arrive home!

10-3/4 oz. can cream of onion
   soup
1/4 c. water
10-oz. pkg. frozen chopped
   spinach, thawed and drained
1 onion, chopped
Optional: 1/4 c. hot peppers,
   chopped

6 boneless center-cut pork chops
salt and pepper to taste
12-oz. pkg. frozen mini potato
   pierogies
Optional: sour cream

In a bowl, mix together soup, water, spinach, onion and peppers, if using. Spread some of soup mixture in the bottom of a large slow cooker. Season pork chops with salt and pepper; arrange over soup mixture. Top with remaining soup mixture. Cover and cook on low setting for 4 hours. Shortly before serving, turn slow cooker to high setting. Add frozen pierogies to slow cooker, pushing them down into sauce. Cover and cook on high setting for about 20 minutes, until pierogies are cooked through. Top pierogies with a little sour cream, if desired. Makes 6 servings.

For best results when cooking in a slow cooker, be sure the crock
is filled at least half full and no more than two-thirds full.

Hungarian Goulash

Kathy Harris
Valley Center, KS

One of my favorite comfort foods...and a filling meal without much effort! Just toss the ingredients into the slow cooker and voilà, you have a wonderful meal for your family.

1-1/2 lbs. stew beef, cubed
1 onion, chopped
2 cloves garlic, crushed
2 T. tomato paste
1 c. water, divided
1 T. Hungarian paprika

1/2 t. salt
1/2 t. pepper
1/4 c. all-purpose flour
1/4 c. sour cream
16-oz. pkg. elbow macaroni, cooked

Place beef in a slow cooker; top with onion and garlic. In a small bowl, combine tomato paste, 1/2 cup water and seasonings; drizzle over beef mixture. Cover and cook on low setting for 8 to 9 hours. Shortly before serving, turn slow cooker to high setting. In a small bowl, mix flour, remaining water and sour cream until smooth; stir into beef mixture. Cook, uncovered, on high setting for 10 to 15 minutes, until slightly thickened. Serve goulash over cooked macaroni. Makes 6 servings.

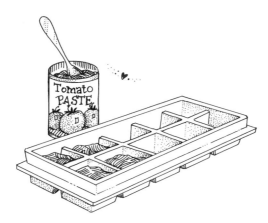

A spoonful or two of tomato paste adds rich flavor to stews and roasts. If you have a partial can left over, freeze the rest in an ice cube tray, then pop out cubes and store in a freezer bag. Frozen cubes can be dropped right into simmering dishes... there's no need to thaw!

Cheesy Potato Puff & Ham Bake *Kathryn Hostetler*
West Farmington, OH

This casserole is delicious any time of year. Serve with homemade chunky applesauce and freshly baked rolls.

1 T. butter
1 c. cooked ham, diced
1/2 c. onion, chopped
2 eggs, beaten
2 c. milk

salt and pepper to taste
3 c. shredded Cheddar cheese, divided
32-oz. pkg. frozen potato puffs, thawed

Add butter to a skillet over medium heat. Add ham and onion; cook until onion is soft. Set aside. In a large bowl, whisk together eggs and milk; add salt and pepper. Stir in ham mixture and 2 cups cheese; fold in potato puffs. Transfer to a buttered 9"x9" baking pan. Top with remaining cheese. Bake, uncovered, at 350 degrees for one hour, or until bubbly and golden. Makes 6 servings.

A diner-style dinner is fun for the whole family! Make placemats from vintage maps, roll up flatware in paper napkins and serve catsup & mustard from plastic squeeze bottles.

Chicken & Mushroom Bake

Kathy Murphy
Spring Hill, TN

*This is a comfort food recipe that my mother made when
I was younger. It still tastes yummy to me. Enjoy!*

1/4 c. butter, sliced
1 c. all-purpose flour
salt and pepper to taste
3 to 3-1/2 lbs. chicken
1 c. sour cream

10-3/4 oz. can cream of
    mushroom or chicken soup
3/4 c. sliced mushrooms
Garnish: paprika

Place butter in a 13"x9" baking pan; melt in a 350-degree oven and
set aside. Mix together flour, salt and pepper in a shallow dish; coat
chicken pieces. Arrange chicken skin-side down in pan. Bake,
uncovered, at 350 degrees for 30 minutes. Stir together sour cream,
soup and mushrooms. Spoon mixture over chicken; sprinkle with
paprika. Bake an additional 30 minutes, or until chicken juices run
clear when pierced. Makes 6 servings.

Make a double batch of your favorite comfort food and invite
neighbors over for supper...what a great way to get to know them
better. Keep it simple with a tossed salad, warm bakery bread and
apple crisp for dessert. It's all about food and fellowship!

White Bean & Ham Soup

Janice Mullins
Kingston, TN

*This quick-to-fix soup is so comforting. Served with a
hot slice of cornbread, it can't be beat!*

1 onion, diced
2 cloves garlic, diced
1 T. olive oil
2 15-oz. cans white beans
12-oz. can evaporated milk

2 14-1/2 oz. cans chicken broth
1 c. cooked ham, diced
1 c. peas
Optional: shredded Cheddar
    cheese

In a deep skillet or saucepan over medium heat, sauté onion and garlic
in olive oil until tender. Stir in undrained beans, milk and broth. Cook
over medium heat until mixture comes to a boil, stirring occasionally.
Stir in ham and peas; reduce heat to low. Simmer until heated through.
Garnish individual servings with cheese, if desired. Makes 6 to
8 servings.

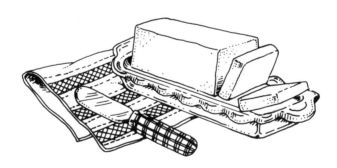

Add a little butter to the oil when sautéing...it helps foods
cook up golden and adds delicious flavor.

Sausage, Bean & Barley Soup

Deborah Thompson
Taswell, IN

Very tasty and satisfying...perfect for cool nights! I usually have the sliced vegetables ready in a container in the refrigerator, all set to add to the soup when I get home.

1 lb. smoked turkey sausage or
    Kielbasa sausage, sliced
    1/4-inch thick
5 c. water
15-1/2 oz. can Great Northern
    beans, drained
14-1/2 oz. can stewed tomatoes
1 onion, chopped

2 stalks celery, sliced
1/2 c. carrot, peeled and coarsely
    chopped
1/2 c. quick-cooking barley,
    uncooked
2 t. Worcestershire sauce
1/2 t. dried basil

Combine all ingredients in a Dutch oven. Bring to a boil over medium-high heat. Reduce heat to medium-low. Cover and simmer for 15 to 20 minutes, until vegetables are tender. Makes 4 to 6 servings.

Soups taste even better the next day...why not make a favorite soup ahead of time? Let it cool thoroughly, then cover and refrigerate until tomorrow night.

Quick Chicken & Corn Chowder

Becky Butler
Keller, TX

This hearty soup can go from stovetop to table in under 30 minutes, yet it tastes like it took all day to make. Round it out with a tossed salad for a satisfying home-cooked meal.

2 T. olive oil
1/4 c. onion, chopped
1/4 c. celery, chopped
Optional: 1 jalapeño pepper,
   seeded and minced
2 T. all-purpose flour
3 c. milk

2 c. cooked chicken, chopped
1-1/2 c. corn
14-3/4 oz. can creamed corn
1/4 t. dried thyme
1/4 t. cayenne pepper, or to taste
1/8 t. salt

Place olive oil, onion and celery in a Dutch oven over medium heat. Add jalapeño pepper, if using. Cook for about 3 minutes, or until vegetables are tender, stirring frequently. Add flour; cook and stir for one minute. Stir in remaining ingredients; bring to a boil. Reduce heat to medium-low and simmer until thickened, about 5 to 10 minutes. Serves 6.

Hearty chowders are perfect for easy weeknight dinners. Make them extra creamy and rich tasting...simply replace the milk or water called for in the recipe with an equal amount of evaporated milk.

Swiss Chard Soup

Eleanor Dionne
Beverly, MA

My father always grew Swiss chard in his garden. Growing up, I never thought I liked it...until I actuallly tasted it! He would cook Swiss chard so many different ways. This soup was one of them.

2 c. beef, chicken or vegetable
    broth
2 c. water
1 potato, peeled and thinly sliced
1 onion, thinly sliced
1 clove garlic, chopped

4 to 5 c. Swiss chard, shredded
    and stalks chopped
1/3 c. country ham, chopped
salt and pepper to taste
Garnish: grated Parmesan
    cheese

Bring broth and water to a boil in a soup pot over medium-high heat. Add potato, onion and garlic. Cook, partly covered, about 15 minutes. Stir in Swiss chard; cook another 10 minutes. Stir in ham, salt and pepper; heat through. Garnish individual servings with Parmesan cheese. Makes 4 servings.

Take time to share family stories and traditions with your kids over the dinner table! A cherished family recipe can be a super conversation starter.

Liz's Hearty Beef Stew

Liz Plotnick-Snay
Gooseberry Patch

I'm always looking for healthy recipes that can cook for up to ten hours while I'm at work. This low-sodium, low-fat recipe is delicious...my husband doesn't even know it's healthy!

1 lb. stew beef, cubed
1 T. all-purpose flour
1/4 t. salt
1/8 t. pepper
2 14-oz. cans Italian-seasoned
   diced tomatoes
1/2 c. red wine or low-sodium
   beef broth
2 c. low-sodium beef broth

1/2 c. water
3 cloves garlic, minced
1 onion, chopped
9-oz. pkg. frozen green beans,
   thawed
9-oz. pkg. refrigerated fettuccine
   pasta, uncooked and cut
   in half

In a plastic zipping bag, toss beef cubes with flour, salt, and pepper; place beef in a slow cooker. Add remaining ingredients except beans and pasta; stir well. Cover and cook on low setting for 9 to 10 hours, until beef is tender. Shortly before serving time, increase heat to high setting. Stir in beans and pasta. Cover and cook on high setting for 8 to 12 minutes longer, until pasta is tender. Makes 4 servings.

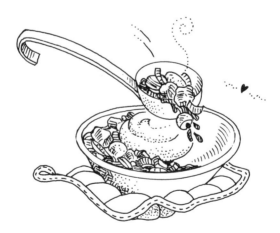

The ultimate comfort food...place a scoop of mashed potatoes in the center of a soup bowl, then ladle hearty stew all around.

Perfect Roast Beef

Tena Stollar
Kensington, OH

This is my go-to beef recipe for the slow cooker...I know I can always count on it for a tender, delicious roast. Often I make it without the vegetables and use the beef as a base for a quick meal. The aroma in the kitchen is so welcoming after I've worked all day.

2 to 3-lb. beef chuck roast
4 potatoes, peeled and cut into
   1-inch cubes
1-1/2 c. carrots, peeled and cut
   into 1-inch chunks

1 onion, quartered
1-1/2 c. beef broth
1-1/2 oz. pkg. vegetable soup
   mix

Place roast in a large slow cooker; surround with vegetables. Combine broth and soup mix in a bowl; pour over roast. Cover and cook on low setting for 6 to 8 hours, or on high setting for 3 to 4 hours, until roast is tender. Serve vegetables with roast. Makes 6 servings.

Mashed & Smashed Potatoes

Jill Ball
Highland, UT

There's nothing more comforting than a huge bowl of mashed potatoes...yum!

2 lbs. redskin potatoes,
   quartered
1/2 c. low-fat cream cheese,
   softened
6 T. low-fat sour cream

1 t. onion powder
3/4 t. salt
1/4 t. pepper
2 T. green onions, diced
Optional: 2 to 4 T. low-fat milk

In a large pot, cover potatoes with water. Bring to a boil over medium-high heat. Cover and simmer until tender, 30 to 40 minutes. Remove from heat; drain completely. Coarsely mash potatoes while still hot, leaving some lumps for texture. In a small bowl, whisk together cream cheese, sour cream and seasonings until smooth. Stir cream cheese mixture and onions into potatoes. Add a little milk if needed to moisten. Season with additional salt and pepper, if desired. Makes 6 servings.

Skillet BBQ Pork Chops

Carol Hummel
Kirkland, WA

I've been making these savory, tender pork chops
for years...comfort food at its finest!

1 T. oil
4 to 6 pork chops
1/3 c. celery, chopped
2 T. brown sugar, packed
2 T. lemon juice

1-1/2 t. dry mustard
1-1/2 t. salt
1/8 t. pepper
2 8-oz. cans tomato sauce

Heat oil in a large skillet over medium heat. Brown pork chops on both sides; drain. Sprinkle celery, brown sugar, lemon juice and seasonings evenly over pork chops. Spoon tomato sauce over all. Cover and simmer over low heat for one hour. Serves 4 to 6.

Rice is a terrific side since it soaks up scrumptious sauce well. Prepare it perfectly...as easy as 1-2-3! One cup long-cooking rice plus 2 cups water equals 3 cups cooked rice. Stir rice into boiling water, cover and simmer over low heat for 20 minutes. Remove from heat. Let stand, covered, a few minutes more, then fluff with a fork.

Lemon Wine Chicken Skillet

Judy Young
Plano, TX

This is one of my family's all-time favorite chicken recipes. It is so easy to make and tastes phenomenal! Serve with steamed rice.

4 boneless, skinless chicken
   breasts
lemon pepper to taste
1 egg
1/2 c. lemon-flavored white
   cooking wine, divided

1/4 c. all-purpose flour
6 T. butter, divided
2 to 3 T. capers
Garnish: chopped fresh parsley

Flatten chicken breasts slightly between 2 pieces of wax paper. Season chicken with lemon pepper. In a small bowl, lightly beat egg with 2 tablespoons wine. Place flour in a separate shallow bowl. Dip chicken in egg mixture, then in flour to coat. Melt 3 tablespoons butter in a large skillet over medium heat; add chicken. Cook until golden on both sides and no longer pink in the center, about 6 minutes on each side. Transfer chicken to a serving dish. Add remaining wine and butter to drippings in skillet; cook and stir until butter melts. Add capers; heat through. To serve, spoon sauce from the skillet over chicken; sprinkle with parsley. Serves 4.

Be sure to use tongs to turn pork chops and chicken in the skillet. Tongs won't pierce the meat like a fork... and all the savory juices will stay inside.

Chicken & Broccoli Bake

Sharon Ninde
Geneva, IN

A scrumptious meal in a pan for two...quick & easy to fix
after a busy day. It's a snap to double the recipe too.

10-oz. pkg. frozen chopped
  broccoli
10-3/4 oz. can cream of chicken
  soup
1/4 c. mayonnaise
1-1/4 t. lemon juice

1/2 t. curry powder
2 c. cooked chicken, cubed
1/2 c. shredded sharp Cheddar
  cheese
1/2 c. soft bread crumbs
2 T. butter, melted

Cook broccoli according to package directions. Drain and place in a
lightly greased 8"x8" glass baking pan. In a saucepan over low heat,
stir together soup, mayonnaise, lemon juice and curry powder until
bubbly; stir in chicken. Spoon mixture over broccoli; top with cheese.
Toss bread crumbs with butter; sprinkle over cheese. Bake, uncovered,
at 350 degrees for 20 minutes, or until golden and heated through.
Serves 2.

Attach vintage porcelain or glass knobs in a row across a length of
wood...just right for keeping tea towels and potholders handy.

Comfort Food Thursday

Pork Chops & Beans Dinner

Linda McGuire
Vinita Park, MO

My mom always fixed this casserole when we were growing up; she said she'd just made it up. It sure tastes good! I've used cream of chicken, asparagus and celery soup, all with tasty results.

10-3/4 oz. can cream of
   mushroom soup
14-1/2 oz. can French-cut
   green beans, drained

4 pork chops
salt and pepper to taste

Combine soup and green beans in an ungreased 2-quart casserole dish. Season pork chops with salt and pepper; arrange on top of soup mixture. Bake, uncovered, at 350 degrees for one hour, until pork chops are cooked through. Serves 4.

Zesty All-Purpose Seasoning

Jenita Davison
La Plata, MO

We love the taste this seasoning gives to pork! It's delicious on chicken too...very good for stovetop cooking and grilling.

1/2 c. orange zest
2 t. onion powder
2 t. dried sage
1 t. dried thyme

1 t. celery salt
1 t. salt
1/2 t. pepper

Combine all ingredients in a food processor; pulse until zest is finely chopped. Store mixture in a covered shaker jar. To use, sprinkle generously on pork or chicken before cooking. For best flavor, let meat stand at least 30 minutes before cooking. Makes about 1/2 cup.

Sour cream will stay fresh and tasty longer if you stir in
a teaspoon or two of white vinegar after first opening it.

Saucy Tuna Squares

Elizabeth Irwin
Eloy, AZ

This has been a favorite dish of mine for a long time.
Add an extra can of tuna if you like. Yummy!

2-1/4 c. biscuit baking mix
1-1/2 c. shredded Cheddar
  cheese, divided
1-1/3 c. milk, divided
6-oz. can tuna, drained
3 to 4 stalks celery, chopped
1/2 c. onion, chopped

2-1/4 oz. can sliced black olives,
  drained
10-3/4 oz. can cream of celery
  or mushroom soup, divided
Optional: 2-oz. jar chopped
  pimentos, drained

In a bowl, toss biscuit mix with 1/2 cup cheese; stir in 2/3 cup milk until a sticky dough forms. Pat dough into a greased 9"x9" baking pan; set aside. In a separate bowl, mix together tuna, celery, onion, olives, half of soup and pimentos, if using. Spoon tuna mixture over dough. Bake, uncovered, at 450 degrees for 25 to 35 minutes. In a saucepan over low heat, combine remaining cheese, milk and soup. Cook until hot and cheese is melted. To serve, cut casserole into squares; ladle sauce over individual squares. Serves 4 to 6.

A crisp green salad goes well with all kinds of main dishes.
For a zippy lemon dressing, shake up 1/2 cup olive oil,
1/3 cup fresh lemon juice and one tablespoon of Dijon mustard
in a small jar. Chill to blend.

Tuna Noodle Casserole

Jennie Gist
Gooseberry Patch

Just the way I remember my grandma making it, topped with crunchy potato chips. We kids usually picked the peas out when she wasn't looking, though!

8-oz. pkg. medium egg noodles, uncooked
10-3/4 oz. can cream of mushroom soup
5-oz. can evaporated milk
1/2 c. sour cream
2 6-oz. cans tuna, drained

4-oz. can sliced mushrooms, drained
1/2 c. peas
1/2 c. onion, minced
Optional: 1 c. potato chips, crushed

Cook noodles according to package directions; drain. In a bowl, combine remaining ingredients except chips. Add noodles; mix well. Pour into a greased 2-quart casserole dish. Top with crushed chips, if using. Bake, uncovered at 350 degrees for 35 to 40 minutes, until hot and bubbly. Makes 4 servings.

Soft bread crumbs tossed with melted butter are a classic crumb topping for casseroles. Crushed tortilla chips, pretzels or savory snack crackers are all tasty too.

Zucchini Yum

Debbie Law
Mascoutah, IL

One day I tossed together some ingredients I had on hand, and this was the delicious result! Sometimes I even enjoy it as a main dish.

1/4 c. butter or olive oil
1 onion, diced
1 zucchini, thinly sliced
1 tomato, diced

Optional: 1 t. garlic, minced
1/2 to 1 c. grated Parmesan
   cheese
salt and pepper to taste

Heat butter or olive oil in a skillet over medium heat. Add onion, zucchini, tomato and garlic, if using. Reduce heat to medium-low; cover and sauté until zucchini is translucent. Sprinkle with Parmesan cheese, salt and pepper; let stand until cheese melts. Serves 2 to 4.

Kentucky Creamed Corn

Jane Guiley
Richmond, KY

Smells and tastes delicious...like fresh corn from the garden!

6 T. butter, sliced
4 c. frozen corn
2 T. all-purpose flour

2 T. sugar
1 t. salt
1/2 c. milk

Add butter and corn to a large saucepan. Cook over low heat until butter is melted and corn is thawed. Add remaining ingredients. Cook and stir until corn is hot and creamy. Serves 8.

Encourage kids to take a no-thank-you helping, or just one bite, of foods they think they don't like...they may be pleasantly surprised!

Tangy Green Beans

Debbie Cutelli
Saint Louis, MO

My husband's mother always requested this dish when she was coming over for dinner. I still think of her whenever I prepare it.

4 slices bacon, cut into 1/2-inch
    pieces
1/2 c. onion, chopped
2 16-oz. cans whole green
    beans, drained

3/4 c. water
3 T. white vinegar
1 cube beef bouillon
1/2 t. pepper

In a large skillet over medium-high heat, cook bacon until lightly browned. Stir in onion; cook until onion is tender. Add remaining ingredients; cook until heated through. Serves 6.

Spicy Garlic Greens

Sheree Beaty
Rochester, NY

Pretty simple and a tasty, healthy side dish! I just kept trying until I got this recipe right for my hubby and myself.

2 bunches collard greens, rinsed
    and torn
14-1/2 oz. can chicken broth
4 cloves garlic, minced

1 t. red pepper flakes
1 t. salt
1/4 t. pepper

Combine all ingredients in a Dutch oven. Bring to a boil over medium-high heat. Reduce heat slightly. Cook until greens are wilted down and cooked through, about 15 minutes. Makes 4 servings.

Serving mashed sweet potatoes for dinner? Add a dash of pumpkin pie spice...yummy!

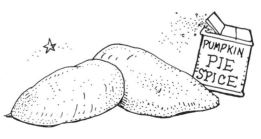

Swedish Meatloaf

Lisa Seckora
Bloomer, WI

After a busy day, this meatloaf is a great comfort food my whole family loves. It's always juicy and delicious...just add mashed potatoes and a vegetable. Leftovers make good sandwiches.

1-1/2 lbs. ground beef
1 egg, beaten
1/2 c. herb-flavored dry bread
   crumbs or stuffing mix

10-3/4 oz. can cream of
   mushroom soup, divided
1/2 c. sour cream
1/4 t. nutmeg

In a large bowl, mix together beef, egg, bread crumbs or stuffing, and half the soup. Form into a loaf; place in a greased 9"x5" loaf pan. Bake, uncovered, at 400 degrees for one hour. At serving time, combine remaining soup, sour cream and nutmeg in a small saucepan; heat over low heat until bubbly. Turn meatloaf out of pan and slice; spoon sauce over slices. Makes 8 servings.

Cut leftover meatloaf into thick slices, wrap individually and freeze. Later, they can be thawed and warmed quickly for scrumptious meatloaf sandwiches at a moment's notice.

Baked Swiss Chicken

Irene Robinson
Cincinnati, OH

Yummy and oh-so easy!

8 boneless, skinless chicken breasts
8 slices Swiss cheese
10-3/4 oz. can cream of chicken soup
1/4 c. white wine or chicken broth
3/4 c. herb-flavored stuffing mix
1/4 c. butter, melted

Arrange chicken in a greased 13"x9" baking pan; top each piece with a slice of cheese. In a bowl, combine soup and wine or broth; mix well and spoon over chicken. Sprinkle with stuffing and drizzle with butter. Bake, uncovered, at 350 degrees for 45 to 50 minutes, until chicken juices run clear when pierced. Makes 8 servings.

Keep a couple of favorite side dishes tucked away in the freezer. Pair with hot sandwiches or a deli roast chicken for a hearty quick meal.

Crunchy Beef & Macaroni

Tiffany Mayberry
Wartburg, TN

The ultimate comfort food...warm, gooey cheese, beef and crunchy French fried onions. No wonder this is my family's favorite dinner!

2 c. elbow macaroni, uncooked
1 lb. ground beef
Optional: 3/4 c. green pepper,
    chopped
3/4 t. seasoned salt

14-oz. can diced tomatoes
10-3/4 oz. can cream of
    mushroom soup
3/4 c. shredded Cheddar cheese
6-oz. can French fried onions

Cook macaroni as package directs; drain. Meanwhile, in a skillet over medium heat, brown beef and drain. Combine macaroni, beef and remaining ingredients except onions; pour into a greased 2-quart casserole dish. Cover and bake at 350 degrees for 30 minutes. Uncover; top with onions and bake 5 minutes longer. Serves 4.

Stock up on favorite pantry items when they're on sale...oh-so handy for homestyle meals in a hurry. Write the purchase date on the package with a permanent marker to make cupboard rotation easy.

Yumm Setta

Christy Albritton
Ava, MO

*I've often made this simple Amish casserole for folks going through
a difficult time. It is a great comfort food. I usually serve it
with garlic bread and sweet corn or a tossed salad.*

16-oz. pkg. wide egg noodles,
   uncooked
10-3/4 oz. can cream of chicken
   soup
1 lb. ground beef
1/2 c. onion, chopped

10-3/4 oz. can tomato soup
salt and pepper to taste
8-oz. pkg. pasteurized process
   cheese spread, cubed and
   divided

Cook noodles as package directs; drain and stir in chicken soup.
Meanwhile, in a skillet over medium heat, brown beef with onion.
Drain; stir in tomato soup, salt and pepper. In a lightly greased 2-quart
casserole dish, layer all of the beef mixture, half of the cheese cubes
and all of the noodle mixture; top with remaining cheese cubes. Bake,
uncovered, at 350 degrees for 30 minutes, or until hot and bubbly.
Serves 4 to 6.

For those who love it, cooking is at once child's play and adult joy.
And cooking done with care is an act of love.

– Craig Claiborne

White Chicken Chili

Mary Rose Kulczak
Noblesville, IN

This hearty chili is delicious! Using a rotisserie chicken is
a terrific shortcut and makes it extra flavorful.

1 onion, chopped	2 c. deli roast chicken, cubed
2 cloves garlic, chopped	4-oz. can diced green chiles
3 T. olive oil	1 t. ground cumin
6 c. chicken broth	salt and pepper to taste
3 16-oz. cans Great Northern	Garnish: sour cream, shredded
beans, drained	Cheddar cheese

In a large stockpot over medium heat, sauté onion and garlic in olive
oil until softened. Stir in remaining ingredients except garnish. Bring to
a low boil, stirring frequently. Reduce heat to low. Cover and simmer
for about 30 minutes, stirring occasionally. Top each bowl with a
dollop of sour cream and a sprinkle of cheese. Serves 4.

Savory Cheese Biscuits

J. C. Schmeltekopf
Johnstown, CO

I've been making biscuits for almost 50 years, since I was ten years
old. I have always loved my cheese biscuits best...they go great with
soups, stews and beans. They are addictive!

2 c. biscuit baking mix	2/3 c. milk
1/2 c. shredded Cheddar cheese	1/4 c. butter, melted
1-1/2 t. dried parsley	1/4 t. garlic powder
1/8 t. garlic salt	

In a bowl, combine biscuit mix, cheese, parsley and garlic salt. Stir in
milk until a soft dough forms. Pat out dough on a floured surface; cut
out 8 biscuits with a round cutter. Press each biscuit into a muffin cup
coated with non-stick vegetable spray. Bake at 425 degrees for 10 to
15 minutes, until golden. Mix butter and garlic powder in a small
bowl; brush over biscuits. Serve warm. Makes 8 biscuits.

Kitchen Cupboard Chili

Nancy Martin
Boise, ID

This chili is a snap to put together...the refried beans are the secret ingredient! Adjust the seasonings to taste as you wish.

1 lb. ground beef
1 c. onion, chopped
16-oz. can red kidney beans, drained
16-oz. can refried beans
8-oz. can tomato sauce

1 T. chili powder
1/2 t. red pepper flakes
1/8 t. cayenne pepper
1 t. garlic powder
1/4 t. pepper
Garnish: saltine crackers

In a large deep skillet or Dutch oven over medium heat, cook beef until no longer pink; drain. In the same skillet, sauté onion until lightly golden. Stir in remaining ingredients except crackers; return beef to skillet. Reduce heat to low; cover and simmer for 30 minutes, stirring occasionally. Serve with crackers. Serves 4.

Crunchy toppings can really add fun and flavor to chili and soup. Some fun and tasty choices...fish-shaped crackers, bacon bits, French fried onions, sunflower seeds and toasted nuts.

Cozy Chicken & Noodles

Sarah Zaouzal
Clermont, FL

I make this simple, creamy skillet recipe for my family all the time. Everyone always asks for seconds, even picky toddlers...serve it and just watch it disappear!

1 onion, chopped
1/2 c. fresh flat-leaf parsley,
   chopped
2 to 3 t. margarine
salt, pepper and onion powder
   to taste
4 boneless, skinless chicken
   breasts

10-3/4 oz. can cream of
   mushroom soup
1 c. milk
8-oz. pkg. wide egg noodles,
   uncooked

In a large deep skillet over medium heat, sauté onion and parsley in margarine until onion is softened. Season with salt, pepper and onion powder. Sauté chicken breasts until golden on both sides; cut into bite-size pieces. Add more salt, pepper and onion powder to chicken, if desired. Continue cooking until chicken is almost cooked through. Stir in soup and milk; bring to a boil. Reduce heat to low and simmer for 30 minutes, stirring occasionally. Meanwhile, cook noodles according to package directions; drain. To serve, ladle chicken mixture over noodles. Makes 4 servings.

Cook egg noodles the easy way...no watching needed. Bring water to a rolling boil, then turn off heat. Add noodles, cover and let stand for 20 minutes, stirring twice.

Hash in a Dash

Moriah Clark
Butler, OH

A terrific quick dish for lunch or dinner. My family even loves to have it for breakfast...we'll eat fresh broccoli any time of day!

3 T. oil
32-oz. pkg. frozen diced
   potatoes, thawed
3 c. cooked ham, cubed
1 t. salt

1/2 t. pepper
2 c. broccoli, cut into bite-size
   flowerets
Garnish: paprika

In a large non-stick skillet, heat oil over medium-high heat. Combine potatoes, ham, salt and pepper in a bowl; add mixture to skillet. Cover and cook for 2 minutes; sprinkle with broccoli. Cover and cook 6 to 8 minutes longer, until potatoes are tender and lightly golden, stirring occasionally. Garnish with a sprinkle of paprika. Makes 6 to 8 servings.

Fill the base of a large hurricane lamp with pretty beach pebbles or colored glass gems, then top with a fat pillar candle for a delightful centerpiece.

Peasant's Beef Pie

Aimee Fanara
Lacona, NY

Good ol' comfort food...it goes together in a jiffy with items you have in your pantry! I call it "peasant food" because my husband cooks excellent, gourmet Italian while I stick to the basics for a simple meal. For another tasty version, use cooked chicken instead of beef and substitute chicken gravy for the mushroom soup.

1 lb. ground beef
2 10-3/4 oz. cans cream of
   mushroom soup
15-oz. can green beans, corn or
   mixed vegetables, drained

Optional: 1/4 c. French fried
   onions, crushed
3 to 4 c. mashed potatoes
1 T. grated Parmesan cheese
Optional: catsup

Brown beef in a skillet over medium heat; drain and set aside. In a bowl, combine soup, vegetables and onions, if using. Add beef and stir well. Spoon into a lightly greased 13"x9" baking pan. Top with large spoonfuls of mashed potatoes; smooth out a little and sprinkle with Parmesan cheese. Bake, uncovered, at 350 degrees for 30 to 40 minutes, until heated through. Drizzle with catsup, if desired. Serves 6 to 8.

Create mini recipe cards listing the ingredients of tried & true dinner recipes. Glue a button magnet on the back and place on the fridge...so handy whenever it's time to make out a shopping list!

Biscuit-Top Chicken Pot Pie

Jane Granger
Manteno, IL

This is a family favorite! You'll love how quick & easy it is.

1 T. butter
10-3/4 oz. can cream of
  chicken soup
10-3/4 oz. can cream of
  mushroom soup
1/2 c. milk
1/2 t. onion powder
1/4 t. dried thyme

1/8 t. pepper
10-oz. pkg. frozen vegetables,
  mixed peas & carrots or lima
  beans, thawed
4 c. cooked chicken, cubed
10-oz. tube refrigerated flaky
  biscuits, quartered

Melt butter in a large skillet over medium heat. Add soups, milk and
seasonings; mix well. Stir in vegetables and chicken; heat through.
Spoon into a lightly greased 13"x9" baking pan. Arrange biscuit pieces
over hot filling. Bake, uncovered, at 375 degrees for 20 to 25 minutes,
until bubbly and biscuits are golden. Makes 6 servings.

Tuck packets of gravy and seasoning mix into a vintage
napkin holder to keep the pantry tidy.

World's Easiest Stuffed Peppers
Julie O'Brien Deasy
New Canaan, CT

This is a great dish for the entire family. I usually make it the day after we've had Chinese take-out, to use up some of the leftover rice we always seem to have. Fresh parsley makes a real difference in the flavor!

4 green peppers, tops removed
1 lb. ground turkey or beef
1/2 to 1 c. cooked brown or
    white rice
1/4 c. grated Parmesan cheese

1/3 c. fresh parsley, chopped
1/2 t. Italian seasoning
1/4 t. salt
1/4 t. pepper
1-1/3 c. marinara sauce, divided

Stand up peppers in a lightly greased 9"x9" baking pan; set aside. In a large bowl, combine meat, rice, cheese, parsley, seasonings and 1/3 cup marinara sauce; mix gently. Stuff peppers with meat mixture; spoon remaining sauce equally over and around peppers. Replace tops of peppers. Bake, uncovered, at 350 degrees for one hour, or until peppers are tender and meat is no longer pink in the center. Makes 4 servings.

To test for doneness, insert the tip of a table knife in the center of a casserole. If the knife tip is hot to the touch when pulled out, the casserole should be heated through. Works for stuffed peppers too!

Ilene's Goulash

Cassandra Gleason
Fond du Lac, WI

A recipe I learned from my dear mother-in-law...it's my husband's favorite meal. Serve with garlic bread and enjoy!

16-oz. pkg. elbow macaroni, uncooked
1 lb. ground beef
1/2 t. onion powder

1/4 to 1/2 t. seasoning salt
46-oz. can tomato juice
1/2 t. salt
1/2 t. pepper

Cook elbow macaroni as directed on package; drain. Meanwhile, in a Dutch oven over medium heat, cook beef until browned. Drain; season with onion powder and seasoning salt. Stir tomato juice into beef mixture; season with salt and pepper. Reduce heat to low; simmer for 10 to 15 minutes. Add macaroni to beef mixture; heat through. Serves 6 to 8.

Speedy homestyle tomato soup for a super-busy night...terrific alongside grilled cheese sandwiches! Combine a can of diced tomatoes with a can of tomato soup and simmer until hot. Add a little milk if you like it creamy. This makes two to three servings, but it's a snap to double it.

Aunt Nada's Salisbury Steak

Judy Schroff
Churubusco, IN

My aunt gave this tried & true recipe to my mother,
who passed it on to me. So good with mashed potatoes!

1-1/2 lbs. ground beef	1 T. all-purpose flour
1/2 c. dry bread crumbs	1/4 c. catsup
1 egg, beaten	1/4 c. water
1/4 t. salt	1 t. Worcestershire sauce
10-3/4 oz. can French onion	1/2 t. mustard
soup, divided	

In a bowl, combine beef, bread crumbs, egg, salt and 1/3 cup soup. Form into 6 oval patties. Brown patties in a skillet over medium heat; drain. In a bowl, stir flour into remaining soup; add remaining ingredients. Pour mixture over patties. Stir to loosen any brown bits in the bottom of the skillet. Cover and cook over low heat for 20 minutes, or until hot and bubbly. Makes 6 servings.

Add the words "You Are Special Today" around the rim of a dinner plate with a glass paint pen. Reserve it for family birthdays and graduations...even for small accomplishments like a child learning to tie her shoes. It's sure to become a cherished tradition.

Buttery Scalloped Potatoes

Karol Cloutier
Alberta, Canada

I had to learn how to cook at a very young age because my mom had polio. This is one of the delicious recipes she taught me to make.

2 T. all-purpose flour
1 t. salt
1/4 t. pepper
4 c. potatoes, peeled and thinly
   sliced

2/3 c. sweet onion, thinly sliced
2 T. butter, sliced
1-1/2 c. milk
Garnish: paprika

Mix together flour, salt and pepper in a cup; set aside. In a greased 2-quart casserole dish, layer half each of potatoes, onion, flour mixture and butter. Repeat layering; set aside. Heat milk just to boiling and pour over top; sprinkle with paprika. Bake, covered, at 375 degrees for 45 minutes. Uncover and bake an additional 10 minutes, or until potatoes are tender and golden. Serves 8.

Dill Potato Wedges

Lori Rosenberg
University Heights, OH

Easy enough for everyday...delicious enough for a holiday!

7 to 8 new redskin potatoes,
   cut into wedges
1/4 c. butter
2 cloves garlic, chopped

2 t. dill weed
1/2 t. salt
1/2 t. pepper
1/4 t. celery salt

Cover potatoes with water in a saucepan. Cook over medium-high heat until soft, about 15 minutes; drain well on paper towels. Melt butter in a large skillet over medium-high heat. Sauté garlic for about one minute. Add potatoes and seasonings to skillet. Cook until golden, stirring often, about 5 minutes. Makes 4 servings.

Separate frozen vegetables in a jiffy...place them in
a colander and run under cold water.

Bratwurst Casserole

Tena Herman
Bucyrus, OH

My hometown is considered the Bratwurst Capital of the USA...our annual three-day Bratwurst Festival attracts over 100,000 people! Most people add cream of mushroom soup to their casseroles, but I don't. I prefer just the taste of the bratwurst and sauerkraut!

8-oz. pkg. thin egg noodles,
   uncooked
16-oz. can sauerkraut, drained
   and liquid reserved
1/2 c. onion, chopped

1 lb. ground pork bratwurst
   or bratwurst links, casings
   removed
1/4 t. pepper
1 t. sugar

Cook noodles according to package directions, using reserved sauerkraut liquid as part of the cooking liquid; drain. Meanwhile, in a skillet over medium heat, brown onion and bratwurst; do not drain. Add pepper and sugar; mix well. Stir in sauerkraut and cooked noodles. Transfer to a lightly greased 13"x9" baking pan. Bake, uncovered, at 350 degrees for 30 minutes. Makes 8 servings.

Spicy Fried Apples

Melody Taynor
Everett, WA

Pure down-home comfort...so tasty with grilled sausage.

1-1/2 lbs. Granny Smith apples,
   cored and cut into wedges
1-1/2 T. sugar

1/4 t. cinnamon
1/4 t. nutmeg
1/4 c. bacon drippings or butter

In a bowl, toss apples with sugar and spices. Heat drippings or butter in a large skillet over medium-high heat. Add apples to skillet. Cook until tender and golden, turning to cook on all sides, about 10 minutes. Serve warm. Makes 6 servings.

Wisconsin Beer Bread

Jerrilynn Atherton
Biloxi, MS

This three-ingredient recipe has been handed down in my family from generation to generation. Now that I live in Texas, it's a touch of home. Bread-making doesn't get much easier than this!

3 c. self-rising flour
3 T. sugar

12-oz. can regular or
non-alcoholic beer

Combine all ingredients in a bowl; stir until moistened. Pour batter into a greased 9"x5" loaf pan. Bake at 350 degrees for 50 minutes to one hour, until crunchy on top. Serve warm. Makes one loaf.

Make mealtime extra special with cloth napkins...pretty place settings too! Simply glue wooden alphabet letter initials to plain napkin rings.

Potluck Macaroni & Cheese

Theresa Wehmeyer
Rosebud, MO

I've often toted this slow-cooker dish to family reunions and church potlucks. Everyone appreciates its creamy goodness, and the pot always comes home empty.

16-oz. pkg. elbow macaroni,
  uncooked
1/2 c. margarine
1/2 c. all-purpose flour
2 t. salt

4 c. milk
16-oz. pkg. pasteurized process
  cheese spread, cubed
Garnish: paprika

Cook macaroni according to package directions; drain. Meanwhile, melt margarine in a saucepan over medium heat. Stir in flour and salt; gradually stir in milk. Cook and stir until thickened. Add cheese; stir until completely melted. Combine cooked macaroni and cheese sauce in a large slow cooker. Top with a sprinkle of paprika. Cover and cook on low setting for 4 hours. Makes 8 to 10 servings.

Fill up a relish tray with crunchy fresh veggies as a simple side dish... add a cup of creamy salad dressing to enjoy as a veggie dip.

Marinated Tomato Salad

Susan Schmirler
Hartland, WI

*This recipe is heavenly year 'round. Give it a try
and I think you'll agree!*

8 tomatoes, sliced
1/2 c. fresh parsley, minced
1/4 c. oil
2 T. tarragon vinegar or cider
    vinegar
1 T. sugar

2 t. mustard
1 clove garlic, pressed
1 t. salt
1/2 t. pepper
Garnish: lettuce leaves

Reassemble the sliced tomatoes, sprinkling parsley between the slices as they're stacked. Place in a glass dish; set aside. Combine remaining ingredients except lettuce in a bowl; drizzle over tomatoes. Cover and refrigerate at least one hour. Before serving, let stand at room temperature 20 minutes. Serve on lettuce leaves, either as whole tomatoes or as slices. Makes 8 servings.

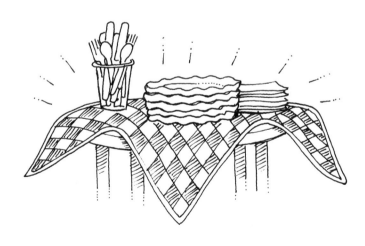

Declare a Picnic Night at home! Just toss a checkered tablecloth on the dinner table and set out paper plates and disposable plastic utensils. Relax and enjoy dinner with no dishes to wash!

Pineapple-Cherry Cake

Dawn Romero
Lewisville, TX

Simply delicious...no one will believe how easy it is to make!

20-oz. can crushed pineapple
18-1/4 oz. pkg. yellow cake mix,
   divided
15-1/2 oz. can pitted cherries,
   drained

1 c. chopped walnuts or pecans
1 c. butter, melted
Optional: ice cream or frozen
   whipped topping, thawed

Evenly spoon pineapple into an ungreased 13"x9" baking pan.
Sprinkle half the cake mix on top; spread cherries over cake mix.
Sprinkle remain-ing cake mix over cherries; top with nuts. Drizzle with
butter; bake at 350 degrees for 45 to 50 minutes. Garnish with ice
cream or whipped topping, if desired. Serves 15.

Children are sure to be helpful in the kitchen when they're
wearing their very own kid-size aprons. Visit a craft store to
select fabric crayons and plain canvas aprons, then let kids
decorate their apron as they like. Follow package directions
to make the design permanent.

Nutty Peach Cobbler

Debbie White
Williamsville, WV

Mom found this recipe in one of her cookbooks. It has been so long, she doesn't remember where she got it. But the first time I made it for an after-church dinner, everyone went crazy for it, and now it is my most-requested dessert. It is almost too easy, only five ingredients. Very, very good!

2 15-oz. cans sliced peaches
18-1/4 oz. pkg. butter pecan
   cake mix

1/2 c. butter, melted
1-1/2 c. shredded coconut
1-1/2 c. chopped pecans

Pour peaches with juice into a greased 13"x9" baking pan. Sprinkle dry cake mix evenly over peaches. Drizzle melted butter evenly over cake mix. Sprinkle coconut and nuts on top. Bake at 350 degrees for 50 to 60 minutes. Makes 8 to 10 servings.

Freeze dollops of whipped cream ahead of time to use for desserts... it's easy. Just drop heaping tablespoonfuls onto a chilled baking sheet and freeze. Remove from the baking sheet and store in a plastic zipping bag. To use, place a dollop on individual dessert portions and let stand a few minutes.

No-Bake Oatmeal Bars

Mary Patenaude
Griswold, CT

We all love chocolatey no-bake drop cookies. This recipe tastes the same but is even easier since it's pressed into a pan!

1/2 c. butter, sliced
1/3 c. milk
3/4 c. honey
1/2 c. baking cocoa

1 t. vanilla extract
1/2 c. creamy peanut butter
3 c. quick-cooking oats,
    uncooked

Mix together butter, milk, honey and cocoa in a saucepan over medium heat; bring to a boil. Boil for 3 minutes, stirring constantly. Remove from heat. Add vanilla and peanut butter; mix well. Stir in oats. Spread into a greased 8"x8" baking pan. Cover and refrigerate until set, 2 to 3 hours. Cut into bars. Makes 2 to 2-1/2 dozen.

For a busy-night dessert, top slices of bakery pound cake with fresh berries and dollops of whipped topping...what could be simpler?

Baked Potato Bar

Louise Graybiel
Ontario, Canada

This recipe is terrific for casual suppers and get-togethers...everyone gets a potato fixed their favorite way, and you don't spend much time in the kitchen! Prepare everything ahead of time, then you can just reheat the potatoes and chili at the last minute.

4 russet potatoes
2 c. chili, warmed
1 c. bacon, crisply cooked and
   crumbled
2 c. shredded Cheddar cheese

2 c. sour cream
1 c. green onions or fresh
   chives, chopped
1 c. green olives with pimentos,
   chopped

Pierce potatoes several times with a fork. Bake at 350 degrees for about one hour, until tender. Cut potatoes in half lengthwise; arrange on a platter. Set out remaining ingredients in separate bowls buffet-style so everyone can choose their own toppings. Serves 4.

Crazy-Good Seasoned Salt

Becky Butler
Keller, TX

We love to use this flavorful blend at the table. Placed in a pretty shaker bottle, it also makes a thoughtful gift for friends.

1/4 c. sea salt
1 t. pepper
1 t. dill weed
1 t. onion powder
1 t. garlic powder
1/2 t. paprika

1/4 t. chili powder
1/4 t. dried sage
1/4 t. dried oregano
1/4 t. dried marjoram
1/4 t. lemon zest

Combine all ingredients in a blender or food processor. Process until finely chopped. Store in a shaker bottle; use like seasoned salt at the stove and dinner table. Makes 1/2 cup.

Build-Your-Own Taco Pizza

Charity Walton
Oxford, IA

So easy and tons of fun for any family gathering. From the super picky to the pile-it-all-on folks, everyone finally gets the toppings they want!

1 lb. ground beef
1-1/4 oz. pkg. taco seasoning
  mix
3/4 c. water
12-inch unbaked pizza crust
15-oz. can refried beans

Garnish: shredded lettuce, shredded cheese, black olives, onions, tomatoes, peppers, sour cream, taco sauce, tortilla chips

Brown beef in a skillet over medium heat; drain. Stir in seasoning mix and water; bring to a boil and simmer for 5 minutes. Meanwhile, place pizza crust on an ungreased baking sheet; prebake, if specified by package directions. Spread beans over crust; spread beef mixture over beans. Bake pizza at 425 degrees for 10 minutes, or until crust is golden. Cool for a few minutes; cut into wedges. Set out toppings of your choice. Makes 6 servings.

Friday night is a great time to invite new neighbors to share a meal. Send them home with a gift basket filled with flyers from favorite bakeries and pizza parlors, coupons and local maps...tuck in a package of homemade cookies too. So thoughtful!

Pizza Butter Muffins

Christine Beauregard
West Swanzey, NH

This yummy create-your-own pizza is fun for any type of gathering. Kids especially enjoy fixing their own. My mom used to make this as a quick after-school snack or Saturday lunch for my five siblings and me. We have all continued the tradition!

1-1/2 c. butter, softened
2 6-oz. cans tomato paste
16-oz. pkg. shredded mozzarella
  cheese
16-oz. pkg. shredded Cheddar
  cheese
1 t. sugar
2 t. dried oregano
garlic powder, salt and pepper to
  taste

10 English muffins, split
Garnish: browned sausage
  or ground beef, crumbled
  bacon, diced ham, sliced
  mushrooms, diced green
  pepper, diced onion, chopped
  broccoli, pineapple tidbits

In a bowl, blend butter, tomato paste, cheeses, sugar and seasonings. Spread desired amount over muffin halves; add desired toppings. Toppings may instead be stirred into butter mixture before spreading over muffins. Place muffins on ungreased baking sheets. Broil until golden and bubbly, about 5 minutes, watching closely to avoid burning. Serves 10.

Invite family & friends over for a Game Night. After enjoying a casual supper together, bring out all the old favorite board games. Don't forget to supply silly prizes and big bowls of buttered popcorn as the evening goes on!

Hamburger "Cupcakes"

Giselda Lok
British Columbia, Canada

One of my favorites! These are so good, they almost taste like a sausage roll. Just add a salad for a satisfying meal.

12 slices white or whole-wheat bread
1/4 to 1/2 c. butter, softened
1 lb. ground beef
1/2 c. onion, chopped
10-3/4 oz. can cream of mushroom soup
1/2 c. shredded sharp Cheddar cheese
salt, pepper and garlic powder to taste
Optional: additional cheese

Cut off the crusts from each bread slice; cut the crusts into cubes and set aside. Spread butter over one side of each bread slice. Press bread, butter-side down, into muffin cups. In a bowl, combine crust cubes and remaining ingredients; mix well. Divide mixture among muffin cups. Top with a little more cheese, if desired. Bake at 375 degrees for 35 to 40 minutes, until no longer pink in the center. Makes one dozen.

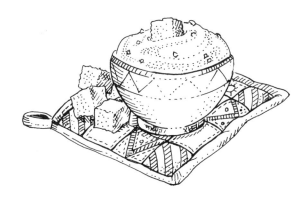

Whip up a creamy veggie dip in a jiffy! Combine one cup cottage cheese, 1/4 cup plain yogurt, one tablespoon minced onion, one teaspoon dried parsley and 1/4 teaspoon dill weed. Blend until smooth; cover and chill to allow flavor to develop.

Cheeseburger Macaroni

Suzanne Bayorgeon
Norfolk, NY

If you're headed out afterward to a ball game or to the movies, you'll love this supper recipe...it's kid-friendly, quick & easy!

1 lb. ground beef
2-1/4 c. water
1/2 c. catsup
1 t. mustard

2 c. elbow macaroni, uncooked
12-oz. pkg. pasteurized process
   cheese spread, cubed

Brown beef in a large skillet over medium heat. Drain; add water, catsup and mustard. Bring to a boil and stir in uncooked macaroni. Reduce heat to medium-low; cover and simmer for 8 to 10 minutes, until macaroni is tender. Add cheese; stir until melted. Serves 4 to 6.

Aunt Pup's Quick Rolls

Becca Brasfield
Burns, TN

My Aunt Pup was famous in our family for not being the greatest cook, but everyone loved her quick & easy rolls. They are simple to make and taste great! The rolls may be made ahead and stored in the refrigerator; just bake them a little longer.

1/2 c. butter, melted
Optional: 1 T. dried, minced
   onion, 1 T. dried parsley,
   1 T. dried chives,
   1/4 t. garlic powder

2 c. biscuit baking mix
8-oz. container sour cream

Place butter in a large bowl; stir in desired seasonings. Add biscuit mix and sour cream; stir just until moistened. Spoon batter into greased muffin cups. Bake at 400 degrees for 15 to 20 minutes, until lightly golden. Serve immediately. May be baked alongside a casserole at 350 degrees for 30 to 35 minutes. Makes one dozen.

A single vintage quilt patch makes a cozy topper for a bread basket...just stitch it to a large napkin in a matching color.

Nightmares

Laura Summers
Greentown, IN

My sister-in-law Roberta used to make these chili beef sandwiches all the time and everyone just loved them. The recipe came from Price's Drive-In in East Saint Louis, Illinois. It's long gone now, but was a hoppin' place back in the 1960s!

1 lb. ground beef
1/2 c. onion, chopped
salt and pepper to taste

15-oz. can chili without beans
8 hamburger buns, split
8 slices American cheese

In a skillet over medium heat, brown beef with onion, salt and pepper; drain. Add chili and mix well; remove from heat. Divide the beef mixture among the bun bottoms; top each with a slice of cheese and bun top. Wrap each bun in aluminum foil; place on a baking sheet. Bake at 350 degrees for 15 to 20 minutes. May be made in advance and frozen unbaked. To serve, bake frozen sandwiches for about 45 minutes. Makes 8 servings.

Let the kids make dinner once a week! Allow them to select the menu and plan the shopping list. With a little help from Mom, they can do the cooking too. You may learn you have a budding chef or two on your hands!

Kid-Pleasin' Chicken Fingers

Nancy Girard
Chesapeake, VA

Much tastier than take-out and oh-so easy to make! Allow
enough time for the chicken to marinate in the buttermilk
mixture for a few hours.

6 boneless, skinless chicken
   breasts, cut into 1/2-inch
   strips
1 egg, beaten
1 c. buttermilk
1-1/2 t. garlic powder

1 c. all-purpose flour
1 c. Italian-flavored dry bread
   crumbs
1 t. baking powder
1 t. salt
oil for deep frying

Place chicken strips in a large plastic zipping bag. In a bowl, whisk
together egg, buttermilk and garlic powder; pour over chicken. Seal
bag and refrigerate for 4 hours, turning occasionally. In a separate
plastic zipping bag, combine remaining ingredients except oil; mix
well. Drain chicken; discard buttermilk mixture. Add chicken to bag
with flour mixture; seal bag and shake to coat. In an electric skillet
over high heat, heat several inches of oil to 375 degrees. Working in
batches, add chicken and fry for 4 to 5 minutes, until golden and
chicken juices run clear. Drain on paper towels. Serves 6.

Best Honey-Mustard Dressing

Denise Winder
Old Fort, TN

My family loves this dressing! It's terrific with chicken fingers
and grilled chicken salad.

1 c. mayonnaise
3/4 c. sour cream

3/4 c. honey
3 T. mustard

Combine all ingredients; mix well. Store, refrigerated, in a covered
container up to 2 weeks. Makes about 2-1/2 cups.

Tracey's Oven-Fried Chicken

Tracey Monnette
Roseville, MI

This is the best baked chicken I've ever tasted! Kids love it too. Use boneless, skinless chicken breasts cut up into nuggets, if you like.

3 to 3-1/2 lbs. chicken
1/2 c. light ranch salad dressing
1 c. dry bread crumbs

garlic powder, onion powder and
pepper to taste

Remove skin from all chicken pieces except wings. Place chicken in a resealable plastic zipping bag. Add salad dressing to bag; seal bag and turn to coat well. Refrigerate at least 30 minutes. Mix bread crumbs with seasonings in a shallow bowl. Drain chicken, discarding salad dressing. Dip chicken pieces into crumb mixture until coated. Arrange on a greased baking sheet; sprinkle any remaining crumb mixture over chicken. Bake at 400 degrees for about 45 minutes, or until chicken juices run clear when pierced. Makes 6 servings.

Watch for whimsical diner-style sectioned plates at tag sales and thrift shops. They're perfect for serving up kid-size portions...and the veggies won't touch the main dish!

Saucy Chicken Drumsticks

Tracey Griego
Tucumcari, NM

Serve with steamed rice, vegetables and plenty of napkins!

3 to 4 lbs. chicken drumsticks
3/4 c. catsup
1/3 c. maple syrup
1/4 c. canola oil

6 T. steak sauce
2 T. chili sauce
2 T. light soy sauce

Remove skin from drumsticks, if desired. Arrange drumsticks in a single layer in a lightly greased 13"x9" baking pan. Mix remaining ingredients in a bowl; pour over drumsticks and toss to coat well. Bake, uncovered, at 375 degrees for 45 to 50 minutes, until chicken juices run clear when pierced. Serves 6 to 8.

Jennifer's Soy Sauce Chicken

Susie Backus
Delaware, OH

This yummy recipe was shared with me by my good friend Jennifer. It's an easy make-ahead dish too, since it needs to be refrigerated at least four hours for the flavor to develop.

12 to 18 chicken drumsticks
1/3 c. brown sugar, packed
1 t. dry mustard

15-oz. bottle soy sauce
1 t. garlic powder

Arrange drumsticks in a greased 13"x9" baking pan; set aside. Mix remaining ingredients in a bowl; pour over drumsticks and toss to coat. Cover and refrigerate 4 hours to overnight, turning chicken over once while marinating. Bake, uncovered, at 375 degrees for one hour and 15 minutes, or until chicken juices run clear when pierced. Serves 6 to 8.

Pick up a dozen pint-size Mason jars...perfect for serving frosty cold beverages at casual get-togethers with family & friends.

Almost-Fried Chicken

Flo Burtnett
Gage, OK

*This is really good and so easy to make. Children can help
by shaking the chicken in the sealed bag.*

3 to 4 T. olive oil
1/2 c. all-purpose flour
1/4 c. cornmeal
1/2 t. paprika
1/2 t. garlic powder

1/2 t. onion powder
1/2 t. salt, or to taste
1/2 t. pepper
4 boneless, skinless chicken
   breasts

Add oil to a 13"x9" baking pan; tilt to coat and set aside. In a large
plastic zipping bag, combine remaining ingredients except chicken;
shake to mix. Add chicken to bag; shake until coated. Arrange chicken
in pan. Bake, uncovered, at 350 degrees for about 45 minutes,
turning several times, until golden and chicken juices run clear.
Makes 4 servings.

Doody's Broccoli Salad

Pat Beach
Fisherville, KY

*My sister Doody shared this recipe with me years ago. It's always
popular at potlucks, showers and family reunions. Our family
really enjoys it...I hope yours will too!*

4 c. broccoli, chopped
8 to 10 slices bacon, crisply
   cooked and crumbled
1/2 c. red onion, chopped
1/2 c. raisins

1 c. mayonnaise-style salad
   dressing
1/3 c. sugar
2 t. vinegar
1 c. sunflower kernels

In a large bowl, combine broccoli, bacon, onion and raisins; set aside.
In a separate bowl, mix together salad dressing, sugar and vinegar.
Drizzle over broccoli mixture and toss to mix well; fold in sunflower
kernels. Cover and chill at least 2 hours before serving. Makes 8 to
10 servings.

Savory Chicken Bundles

Lanie Christiansen
Toledo, OH

*This is a special treat for my family when it's just the four of us
and we're all home for the evening. It's oh-so delicious
and fun for kids to help.*

1 lb. boneless, skinless chicken
  breasts, cooked and chopped
  or shredded
6 slices bacon, crisply cooked
  and crumbled
8-oz. pkg. cream cheese,
  softened

1/3 c. milk
1/4 c. onion, diced
1/4 c. celery, diced
2 8-oz. tubes refrigerated
  crescent rolls

In a bowl, mix together all ingredients except crescent rolls; set aside.
Unroll dough and separate into 4 squares of 2 triangles each, pinching
together seams between triangles. Spoon filling equally into the center
of each square. Bring all 4 corners of each square together above the
filling; twist together and pinch edges to seal. Place bundles on an
ungreased baking sheet. Bake at 325 degrees for about 25 minutes.
Serves 4.

Stock up on festive party napkins, plates and candles at post-holiday
sales. Tuck them away in a big box...you'll be all set to turn any
casual meal or get-together into a party!

Just For Fun Friday

Chicken-Apple Sliders

Katie Majeske
Denver, PA

I love slider sandwiches! They are just the right size, especially when paired with salads and sides. This is one of our favorites.

1 Granny Smith apple, cored and
   shredded
1/4 c. celery, finely chopped
1/2 t. poultry seasoning
1/4 t. pepper
1/4 t. salt
2 T. honey
1 lb. ground chicken

8 slices bacon, crisply cooked,
   crumbled and divided
Optional: 2 slices favorite
   cheese, quartered
8 mini rolls, toasted and split
Garnish: mayonnaise, shredded
   lettuce, sliced tomato and
   onion

In a large bowl, combine apple, celery and seasonings; toss to mix. Add honey, chicken and half of bacon. Stir until combined; do not overmix. Form into 8 small patties. Grill or pan-fry patties about 4 minutes on each side, until chicken is no longer pink. If desired, top with a piece of cheese during the last few minutes of cooking. Place patties on rolls; top with remaining bacon and other toppings, as desired. Makes 8 servings.

Bite-size mini sandwiches make an easy, tasty addition to any casual dinner or party buffet. Whip up some grilled cheese, BLT, Reuben or other favorite sandwiches, then cut them into small squares. Top with an olive or a pickle slice and spear with party picks.

German Burgers

Elizabeth Blackstone
Racine, WI

If you like Reuben sandwiches, you'll love these hamburgers! Can't find pumpernickel buns? Sandwich the burgers between toasted slices of pumpernickel bread. Add a side of hot German potato salad and a dill pickle for a yummy meal with oom-pah-pah!

1-1/2 lbs. ground beef
1/2 c. soft pumpernickel bread
   crumbs
2 T. beer or beef broth
1 T. mustard
1/2 t. caraway seed
1/2 t. salt

1/8 t. pepper
6 slices Swiss cheese
6 pumpernickel sandwich buns,
   split
14-1/2 oz. can sauerkraut,
   drained
Garnish: additional mustard

In a large bowl, combine all ingredients except cheese, buns and sauerkraut. Mix gently and form into 6 patties. Grill or pan-fry patties until no longer pink, about 10 to 15 minutes, turning halfway through. Top with cheese; let stand until cheese melts. Grill buns, if desired. Serve burgers on buns; top with sauerkraut and mustard. Serves 6.

A tasty apple coleslaw goes well with German Burgers. Simply toss together a large bag of coleslaw mix and a chopped Granny Smith apple. Stir in coleslaw dressing or mayonnaise to desired consistency.

Bavarian Wiener Bake

Merikay Daugherty
North Baltimore, OH

My mother made this tasty dish when I was growing up, then I made it for my children. Now my grandchildren are enjoying it too! It's a great way to use up leftover mashed potatoes.

27-oz. can sauerkraut, drained
10-3/4 oz. can cream of
　mushroom soup
1/2 c. mayonnaise, divided
1 t. caraway seed

4 c. mashed potatoes
1 lb. hot dogs, quartered
1/2 c. soft bread crumbs
1 T. butter, melted
1/4 t. paprika

In a bowl, mix together sauerkraut, soup, 1/4 cup mayonnaise and caraway seed; set aside. In a separate bowl, mix potatoes and remaining mayonnaise. Layer potato mixture, sauerkraut mixture and half of hot dogs in a lightly greased 13"x9" baking pan. Combine crumbs, butter and paprika; sprinkle on top. Top with remaining hot dogs. Bake, uncovered, at 350 degrees for 30 to 35 minutes, until heated through. Makes 6 to 8 servings.

Quick-cooking smoked sausage links are a great choice for weeknight meals. Different flavors like hickory-smoked or cheese-filled sausage can really jazz up a recipe too.

Melissa's Hawaiian Chicken

Melissa Hall
East Burke, VT

A fast and easy slow-cooker recipe...great for when you want to come home to a hot meal. My husband says it tastes like Chinese sweet-and-sour chicken. I created this dish with items I had on hand, and now it's a family favorite.

1 to 2 lbs. boneless, skinless
   chicken breasts
1 c. Hawaiian-style marinade
1 red pepper, thinly sliced

20-oz. can crushed pineapple
1/8 t. ground ginger
cooked rice

Place chicken in a slow cooker; top with remaining ingredients except rice. Cover and cook on low setting for 6 to 8 hours. Serve over cooked rice. Makes 4 to 8 servings.

A tropical-themed dinner is a sure cure for chilly-weather cabin fever. Scatter seashells and sand dollars on the table and twine dollar-store flower leis around the place settings...or the diners!

Teriyaki Pot Roast

Gayla Reyes
Hamilton, OH

*My mom has been making this slow-cooker teriyaki beef for years.
It is always requested for family gatherings. Your house
will smell delicious!*

2 to 3 t. oil
3 to 4-lb. beef chuck roast
2 onions, sliced
1/2 c. water

1/4 c. soy sauce
2 to 3 t. garlic, minced
3/4 t. ground ginger

Heat oil in a large skillet or Dutch oven over medium-high heat. Brown roast for about 5 minutes on each side; drain. Add roast to a large slow cooker; top with onions. Combine remaining ingredients in a small bowl; pour over roast. Cover and cook on low setting for 6 to 8 hours, until beef is tender. Makes 6 to 8 servings.

Good china, cloth napkins and lit candles aren't only for holidays and special celebrations...use them to brighten everyday meals!

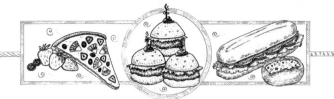

Broccoli Beef Stir-Fry

Diana Chaney
Olathe, KS

My son likes the taste of Chinese pepper steak, but won't eat the green peppers. Now I make it with broccoli instead, and he's joined the clean plate club!

.87-oz. pkg. brown gravy mix
1 c. water
1/4 t. pepper
1 T. oil
3/4 to 1 lb. beef flank steak, sliced into thin strips

2 c. broccoli, cut into bite-size flowerets
cooked rice or linguine pasta
Optional: soy sauce

Whisk together gravy mix, water and pepper in a bowl; set aside. Heat oil in a large skillet over medium-high heat. Add beef strips; cook and stir for 3 to 4 minutes. Stir in broccoli and gravy; bring to a boil. Reduce heat to low; cover and simmer 5 to 8 minutes, or until broccoli is crisp-tender. Serve over cooked rice or pasta, with soy sauce if desired. Makes 4 servings.

Karen's Cucumber Salad

Karen Hilliard
Norfolk, VA

I love Asian food...tempura, sushi, you name it. Over the years, I have tried to recreate the cucumber salad that accompanied some of our favorite dinners out. We really enjoy this salad!

4 cucumbers, peeled and very thinly sliced
2-inch slice fresh ginger, peeled and grated

juice of 1 orange
1/2 c. cider vinegar
1 T. brown sugar, packed
1/4 t. celery seed

In a bowl, combine cucumbers, ginger and orange juice; toss to mix. Add remaining ingredients. Stir gently until blended and brown sugar is dissolved. Cover and refrigerate for one hour. Stir just before serving. Makes 4 to 6 servings.

Chicken & Asparagus Stir-Fry

April Jacobs
Loveland, CO

I can whip up this delicious dish in a lot less time than it'd take us to go out for Chinese food. It's easier on the wallet too.

2-1/2 T. all-purpose flour, divided
1/4 t. salt
1/4 t. pepper
1 lb. boneless, skinless chicken breasts, cubed
2 t. oil
1 c. chicken broth

1-1/2 t. garlic, minced
1/2 lb. asparagus, cut into 1-inch lengths
1 c. cherry tomatoes, halved
2 T. green onions, sliced
2 T. fresh dill, snipped
cooked rice or Asian noodles

In a plastic zipping bag, mix 2 tablespoons flour, salt and pepper. Add chicken; shake to coat. Heat oil in a skillet over medium-high heat. Cook and stir chicken for 4 to 5 minutes, until cooked through. Remove to a plate; cover to keep warm. Blend remaining flour, broth and garlic in a bowl; set aside. Add asparagus to skillet; cook and stir for one minute, or until bright green. Stir in broth mixture; cook for one minute, or until slightly thickened and asparagus is tender. Stir in chicken and tomatoes; remove from heat. Stir in onions and dill. Serve over cooked rice or noodles. Makes 4 servings.

Stir up a simple rice pilaf. In a saucepan, bring 2 cups chicken broth to a boil. Stir in one cup long-cooking rice; reduce heat, cover and simmer for 20 to 25 minutes. Meanwhile, sauté 1/2 cup each sliced mushrooms and green onions in a little oil, just until tender. When rice is done, stir in mushroom mixture, a dash of soy sauce and 1/2 cup snipped fresh parsley; fluff with a fork. Serves 4.

Chinese Chicken Wings

Laura Cline
Ridgely, MD

Years ago, when I was a young girl, I found a teeny-tiny recipe in a magazine. It sounded yummy so I clipped it out. Years later, I've made these wings a hundred times and everyone raves about them! They are so easy to make. They travel well for parties too, just toss them in a covered dish with all the juices and reheat them quickly to serve. I hope you enjoy them as much as my family does.

3 lbs. chicken wings
2 T. olive oil
salt and pepper to taste
1 c. honey

1/2 c. dark soy sauce
2 T. catsup
1 clove garlic, minced

Arrange chicken wings in a single layer on an ungreased, aluminum foil-lined large rimmed baking sheet. Drizzle olive oil sparingly over wings; season with salt and pepper. Mix remaining ingredients in a small bowl; drizzle mixture over wings. Bake, uncovered, at 375 degrees for 20 minutes. Remove from oven; turn wings over, one at a time. Return to oven and bake for another 25 minutes, or until wings have turned a beautiful dark caramel color. Watch closely toward the end of baking time to avoid burning. Serves 4 to 6.

Feeding a crowd? Serve festive Mexican, Italian or Chinese-style dishes that everybody loves. They usually feature rice or pasta, so they're filling yet budget-friendly. The theme makes it a snap to put together the menu and table decorations too.

Ritzy Chicken Wings

Vickie
Gooseberry Patch

A scrumptious and different way to fix chicken wings. Terrific for parties, or serve over rice for a casual meal.

1/4 c. butter, melted
3/4 c. round buttery crackers,
   finely crushed

3/4 c. grated Parmesan cheese
1 t. garlic salt
3 lbs. chicken wings

Place melted butter in a shallow bowl; set aside. In a separate shallow bowl, combine remaining ingredients except chicken wings. Dip wings in butter; roll in crumb mixture to coat. Arrange wings in a single layer on an ungreased large rimmed baking sheet. Bake, uncovered, at 375 degrees for 35 to 40 minutes, until golden and chicken juices run clear when pierced. Serves 4 to 6.

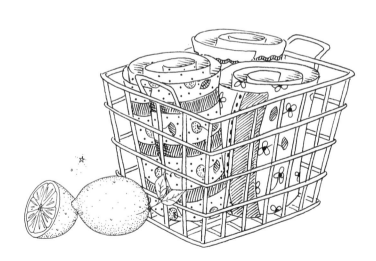

Be sure to set out a tray of warm, moistened towels whenever sticky or messy finger foods are on the menu. Dampen fingertip towels in water and a dash of lemon juice, roll up and microwave on high setting for 10 to 15 seconds. Certain to be appreciated!

Slow-Cooked Pork Ribs

Sara Tatham
Plymouth, NH

Some of the tastiest ribs you'll ever eat! Great with mashed potatoes and coleslaw for a warming winter meal...wonderful with potato salad and corn on the cob for a summertime picnic. A family favorite!

3 to 4 lbs. country-style pork
    ribs, cut into 4 to 6 pieces
Montreal steak seasoning or
    lemon pepper to taste

1 c. barbecue sauce

Sprinkle pork generously with seasoning; place in a large slow cooker. Cover and cook on low setting for 8 to 9 hours, or on high setting for 4 to 5 hours. About 30 minutes before serving, drain liquid from slow cooker; spread barbecue sauce over pork. Cover and continue to cook until warmed through. Serves 4 to 6.

Country Ribs in the Crock

Margie Kirkman
High Point, NC

If you love ribs and like easy recipes, this tasty slow-cooker recipe is just for you.

4 lbs. country-style pork ribs,
    cut into 6 to 8 pieces
1/2 c. apricot jam

1 T. soy sauce
1-1/2 c. barbecue sauce, divided

Place pork in a large slow cooker. In a bowl, combine apricot jam, soy sauce and 3/4 cup barbecue sauce; spoon mixture over pork. Cover and cook on low setting for 8 to 9 hours. Stir in remaining sauce 15 minutes before serving. Cover and cook until warmed through. Makes 6 to 8 servings.

My Mom's Coleslaw

Sarah Oravecz
Gooseberry Patch

This coleslaw rocks! I have made it for potlucks and gotten lots of compliments. Since it keeps well, it's really convenient for making ahead.

1 head cabbage, shredded and
    divided
1 green pepper, chopped
1 red pepper, chopped
1 onion, chopped
1 c. plus 1 T. sugar, divided

1 c. white vinegar
3/4 c. oil
1 T. dry mustard
1 T. celery seed
1 T. salt

In a large bowl with a tight-fitting lid, layer vegetables as follows: half the cabbage, green pepper, red pepper, onion and remaining cabbage. Pour one cup sugar over the top; do not stir. In a small saucepan over medium heat, mix together remaining sugar and other ingredients. Bring to a rolling boil; cool slightly and pour over cabbage mixture. Cover tightly without stirring; refrigerate overnight. Mix well before serving. May be kept refrigerated up to 2 weeks. Serves 16.

Keep a picnic basket packed with a blanket, tableware and other picnic supplies. You'll be ready to pack up an easy-to-tote dinner, load everyone into the car and take off for a picnic at a moment's notice!

Applesauce Pulled Pork

Melissa Rushing
Rogersville, MO

My kids say this slow-cooker pulled pork is as good as what our local barbecue restaurant serves...or better! It's terrific for busy days. In the morning, just fill the crock, and when you arrive home, it's waiting for you to enjoy!

3 to 4 lbs. country-style pork
   ribs, cut into 6 pieces
salt and pepper to taste
1 c. cinnamon applesauce

18-oz. bottle barbecue sauce
Optional: 6 sandwich buns, split

Season pork with salt and pepper; arrange in a large slow cooker. Spoon applesauce and barbecue sauce over pork. Cover and cook on low setting for 8 hours, or until very tender. Pull pork apart with 2 forks. Serve on sandwich buns, if desired. Makes 6 servings.

Mini versions of favorite hot sandwiches are oh-so appealing... diners with light appetites can take just one, while those with heartier tastes can sample two or three. Try using small sandwich rolls or brown & serve dinner rolls instead of full-size buns.

Ground Beef Barbecue

Connie Blakey
Russell Springs, KY

I got this sandwich recipe from my sister 40 years ago...it turned out to be a real keeper! It's one of those recipes that tastes even better the next day.

1-1/2 lbs. lean ground beef	1 T. sugar
1 onion, chopped	1 T. mustard
1/2 c. catsup	1 t. paprika
1/2 c. water	1/4 t. salt
1/4 c. Worcestershire sauce	1/2 t. pepper
1/4 c. red wine vinegar	6 hamburger buns, split
1 T. butter	Garnish: pickle slices

In a large saucepan over medium heat, combine all ingredients except buns and pickles. Bring to a boil; turn heat down to low. Simmer for one hour, stirring occasionally to break up beef. To serve, spoon onto buns; top with pickles. Serves 6.

At the end of the week, turn leftovers into a buffet-style meal. Set out individual servings of casseroles in pretty dishes, toss veggies into a salad and add a basket of warm rolls. Arrange everything on a counter...everyone is sure to come looking for his or her favorites!

Sausage & Pepper Heroes

Sheila Rothmann
North Port, FL

My family loves these zesty sausage sandwiches! This mixture is delicious ladled over cooked pasta too.

2 T. olive oil
4 Italian pork sausage links,
  removed from casings
1 green pepper, sliced
1 onion, sliced
1 clove garlic, minced

1 T. Italian seasoning
1 t. salt
1/2 t. pepper
1 T. red wine vinegar
Optional: 1 c. marinara sauce
4 hero or sub buns, split

Heat olive oil in a large skillet over medium heat. Add sausage and cook until browned, breaking up with a spatula; drain. Add green pepper, onion, garlic and seasonings; cook until vegetables are tender. Stir in vinegar and marinara sauce, if using; heat through. To serve, spoon sausage, pepper and onion onto buns. Makes 4 servings.

Just for fun, spear a cherry tomato or a tiny sweet pickle with a long toothpick and use as a garnish for overstuffed sandwiches.

Saucy Meatball Subs

Kelly McLaughlin
Amherst, OH

Teens as well as adults enjoy these yummy sandwiches topped
with a simple but scrumptious sauce.

1 lb. ground beef sirloin	1/2 to 3/4 c. water
1 onion, grated	1 egg, beaten
dried parsley, dried oregano and	1 c. all-purpose flour
dried basil to taste	oil for frying
salt and pepper to taste	4 sub buns, split
3 slices bread	

In a large bowl, combine beef, onion and seasonings; set aside. In a separate bowl, soak bread with water; squeeze out excess water. Add moistened bread and egg to beef mixture; work mixture together with your hands. With floured hands, form into 12 meatballs. Roll meatballs in flour to coat. Add one inch of oil to a large heavy skillet; heat over medium-high heat until hot. Add meatballs, one at a time, keeping oil hot. Brown for about 7 to 10 minutes on both sides, until cooked through, allowing a crust to form. Stir meatballs into simmering Sub Sauce; heat through. To serve, place several meatballs with some pepper and onion on each bun; spoon any additional sauce on top. Makes 4 servings.

Sub Sauce:

15-oz. can tomato sauce	1 onion, thinly sliced
1 green pepper, thinly sliced	pepper to taste

Place all ingredients in a large skillet or saucepan. Simmer over medium-low heat until vegetables are tender, stirring often.

Sweet potato fries are deliciously different! Slice sweet potatoes into strips or wedges, toss with olive oil and place on a baking sheet. Bake at 400 degrees for 20 to 30 minutes, until tender, turning once. Sprinkle with a little cinnamon-sugar, if you like.

Dad's Wimpy Burgers

Karen DeSantis
Lockport, NY

My father made these tasty burgers often at home. Many years ago, he was a cook at a Civilian Conservation Corps camp in Pennsylvania, where he often made them for his commander. Sadly, Dad has been gone since 1999, but he lives on in his recipes. I still make these burgers for my husband and son.

2 lbs. ground beef
1/2 c. catsup
1 egg, beaten
1 onion, chopped

1 t. salt
1 c. Italian-flavored dry bread
   crumbs
6 to 8 hamburger buns, split

In a large bowl, combine beef, catsup, egg, onion and salt; mix well. Form into 6 to 8 patties; flatten to desired thickness. Place bread crumbs in a shallow pan. Pat each side of patties in crumbs until coated. Place patties in a lightly greased 13"x9" baking pan. Bake, uncovered, at 350 degrees for 20 to 25 minutes, turning over after 8 minutes. Patties may also be pan-fried in a lightly greased skillet over medium heat. Cook on each side for 6 to 8 minutes, until lightly browned. Serve on buns. Makes 6 to 8 servings.

A muffin tin makes a terrific condiment server. Fill each of the cups with something different...catsup, mustard, relish, hot sauce, horseradish and pickle slices are all ideal toppings for sandwiches and burgers.

Beth's Stuffed Burgers

Heather Strauss
Waynesboro, PA

*My sister Beth developed this recipe one day on a whim...
it's been a family favorite ever since!*

2 lbs. lean ground beef
2 eggs, beaten
1/2 c. dry bread crumbs
1/2 c. onion, finely chopped
1/2 c. finely shredded Cheddar
  cheese

1/4 to 1/2 c. barbecue sauce
8 hamburger buns, split and
  toasted
Garnish: favorite toppings

In a large bowl, mix all ingredients except rolls and garnish. Do not overmix. Form into 8 flattened patties. Coat a skillet with non-stick vegetable spray; heat over medium heat. If grilling, place aluminum foil on a rack and coat well with non-stick spray. Add patties and cook for about 5 to 6 minutes on each side, until juices run clear; don't move or press down on patties. Serve patties on toasted buns with desired toppings. Makes 8 servings.

Make a potato print tablecloth...crafty fun for the kids! Cut a potato in half and let them draw simple designs like stars or flowers on the cut surfaces. Cut around the designs with a blunt knife, then pour fabric paint into a paper plate and let 'em stamp away on a plain tablecloth.

Meatball Surprise

Denissa Churchwell
Brownfield, TX

My husband and kids are very happy when I make these meatballs. They taste so good...and the kids love it when the cheese inside oozes out!

1 lb. ground beef
1/2 green pepper, diced, or 4-oz.
   can diced green chiles
1/2 onion, diced

salt and pepper to taste
15-oz. can tomato sauce, divided
3 sticks string cheese, cut into
   thirds

In a bowl, mix beef, green pepper or chiles, onion, salt and pepper together with your hands. Add enough tomato sauce to moisten; mix lightly. Divide beef mixture into 9 flattened patties. Wrap each patty around a piece of cheese to form a ball. Place meatballs in a large skillet; pour remaining tomato sauce over top. Cook over medium heat until well browned. Serve meatballs topped with sauce from skillet. Serves 4.

Fabulous Fries

Wendy Lee Paffenroth
Pine Island, NY

Yum...you'll love this new way to make fries!

2 lbs. potatoes, peeled and cut
   into 1/4-inch strips

1 to 1-1/2 c. light Italian salad
   dressing

Place potatoes in a bowl; drizzle with salad dressing and stir to coat. Transfer to a 13"x9" baking pan coated with non-stick vegetable spray. Bake, uncovered, at 325 degrees for 12 to 15 minutes; turn with a spatula. Bake an additional 10 minutes, or until crisp and golden. Makes 6 to 8 servings.

Heaven give you many, many merry days!
– William Shakespeare

Just For Fun Friday

Old-Time Coney Dogs

Debra Arch
Kewanee, IL

Who doesn't love coney dogs like you can get at the county fair?
They're so easy to fix in a slow cooker, so treat your family!

1/2 lb. ground beef
1/4 c. onion, chopped
8-oz. can tomato sauce
3/4 t. garlic powder

1 t. chili powder
1/2 t. salt
6 hot dogs
6 hot dog buns, split

Brown beef and onion in a skillet over medium heat. Drain; stir in tomato sauce and seasonings. Spoon into a slow cooker; place hot dogs on top. Cover and cook on low setting for 5 to 6 hours. To serve, partially split each hot dog down the center; place on a bun and top with some of the beef mixture. Makes 6 servings.

Kansas City BBQ Beans

Wendy O'Hara-Reaume
Ontario, Canada

Growing up in Kansas City, barbecue was a major part of our menu.
My husband loves smoked food like bacon, so I came up with this
recipe to please him...sweet, saucy barbecue love!

4 15-oz. cans baked beans
1/2 lb. bacon, crisply cooked and
    crumbled
1 onion, diced
1 c. dark brown sugar, packed

18-oz. bottle Kansas City-style
    or mesquite barbecue sauce
1 t. smoke-flavored cooking
    sauce
1/2 t. pepper

Place all ingredients in a lightly greased 13"x9" baking pan; stir until combined. Cover tightly with aluminum foil. Preheat a grill to medium-low. Place pan on grill for 20 minutes, stirring every 5 minutes to prevent scorching. Remove foil and grill another 5 to 10 minutes, until thickened. May also be baked in the oven at 400 degrees for 30 minutes; no need to stir. Uncover and bake another 5 to 10 minutes, until thickened. Serves 8 to 10.

Duchess Dogs

Lois Long-Crane
Kingston, WA

My mom used to make this dish, and my sons loved it when they were growing up. From the list of simple ingredients, you'd never guess how good it is!

1/2 c. onion, diced
5 T. butter
3 c. boiling water
1-1/4 c. cold milk
8-oz. pkg. instant mashed
   potato flakes

1 egg, beaten
1 lb. all-beef hot dogs
1/2 c. shredded Cheddar cheese

In a saucepan over medium heat, sauté onion in butter. Add boiling water to pan; remove from heat. Add milk; stir in potato flakes. Cool slightly; stir egg into potatoes. Meanwhile, simmer hot dogs in a saucepan of boiling water until heated through. Put hot dogs in a lightly greased 13"x9" baking pan and partially split them lengthwise. Spoon mashed potatoes evenly into hot dogs; sprinkle with cheese. Bake, uncovered, at 350 degrees for about 15 minutes, until cheese is melted. Serves 4 to 8.

Kristy's Zucchini Sticks

Kristy Markners
Fort Mill, SC

I've taste-tested fried zucchini sticks at a restaurant. These are much healthier for you and taste better too!

2 egg whites
1 c. Italian-flavored panko bread
   crumbs
1/4 t. cayenne pepper
1/4 t. seafood seasoning
1/4 t. salt

1 to 2 zucchini, cut into
   1/4-inch strips
Garnish: grated Parmesan cheese
Optional: ranch dressing for
   dipping

Beat egg whites in a shallow bowl until foamy. Combine bread crumbs and seasonings in a separate shallow bowl. Toss zucchini strips in egg whites, then in bread crumbs to coat. Place on a baking sheet coated with non-stick vegetable spray. Sprinkle with Parmesan cheese; spray tops lightly with non-stick spray. Bake at 450 degrees for 15 to 20 minutes, until crisp and golden. Serves 6.

Baked Beanies & Weenies

Andrea Ford
Montfort, WI

This recipe was my mother's. I remember her making it for a fast supper after we had been working outside all day. This dish has excellent flavor, and it's really quick to fix.

2 16-oz. cans pork & beans
6 to 8 hot dogs
2 T. brown sugar, packed

1 t. mustard
1 t. Worcestershire sauce

Pour beans into a lightly greased shallow 11"x8" baking pan. Slash hot dogs diagonally and arrange on top of beans, cut-side up. In a small bowl, combine remaining ingredients; spread over hot dogs. Bake, uncovered, at 450 degrees for 20 minutes, or until hot and bubbly. Serves 6.

Stir up a pitcher of pink lemonade for a casual meal. Combine 3 cups water, 1/2 cup sugar and 1/2 cup lemon juice. Stir until sugar dissolves and add a little maraschino cherry juice to tint it pink. Serve over ice.

Upside-Down Pizza Casserole

Margaret Stears
Burr Ridge, IL

My grandchildren really like this dish!

1 lb. ground beef
1 c. onion, chopped
1 c. green pepper, chopped
15-oz. can pizza sauce
1/2 c. sliced pepperoni, chopped

1/2 t. Italian seasoning
6-oz. pkg. thinly sliced
  mozzarella cheese
1/2 c. grated Parmesan cheese

In a skillet over medium heat, brown beef, onion and green pepper; drain. Stir in pizza sauce, pepperoni and seasoning; simmer over low heat for 10 minutes. Spoon beef mixture into a greased 13"x9" baking pan. Place mozzarella cheese slices over hot beef mixture. Pour Batter Topping over cheese; sprinkle with Parmesan cheese. Bake, uncovered, at 400 degrees for 20 to 30 minutes, until puffed and golden. Serves 6 to 8.

Batter Topping:

2 eggs, beaten
1 c. milk
1 T. oil

1 c. all-purpose flour
1/2 t. salt
1/2 c. grated Parmesan cheese

Combine eggs, milk and oil in a bowl; whisk for one minute. Add remaining ingredients; stir until smooth.

Take it easy on alternate Friday nights...arrange for a friendly dinner swap! One week, you make a double batch of a favorite casserole and deliver one to a friend. Next week, she returns the favor. You're sure to discover some great new recipes while gaining a little free time too.

Lori's Pizza Roni

Lori West
Bethel, OH

*I've been making this recipe for 30 years! My kids still love it,
and now that they're grown, they make it for their own families.
We hope you'll enjoy it too.*

16-oz. pkg. elbow macaroni or
   small seashell macaroni,
   uncooked
1 lb. ground beef or turkey
1 to 2 15-oz. jars pizza or
   spaghetti sauce

Optional: sliced pepperoni
8-oz. pkg. shredded mozzarella
   cheese

Cook macaroni according to package directions; drain and place in a
lightly greased 13"x9" baking pan. Meanwhile, brown meat in a skillet
over medium heat; drain. Spoon meat and desired amount of sauce
over macaroni. Stir gently and spread evenly in pan. If desired, arrange
pepperoni slices over top. Cover with cheese. Bake, uncovered, at
350 degrees for 30 minutes, or until cheese is melted and golden.
Serves 4 to 6.

Serve up some tasty soft pretzels instead of dinner rolls. Twist strips
of refrigerated bread stick dough into pretzel shapes (or let the kids
do it!) and place on an ungreased baking sheet. Brush with beaten
egg white, sprinkle with coarse salt and bake as the package directs.

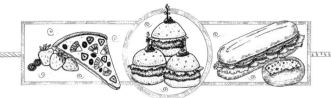

Baked Omelet Your Way

James Bohner
Harrisburg, PA

My wife likes eggs one way and I like them another, so we make this half & half...it's more fun, especially for our kids! Speed up mealtime by using frozen diced veggies and a jar of real bacon bits.

4 slices bread, toasted and cubed
8 eggs, beaten
4 c. milk
2 c. shredded Cheddar cheese, divided
1/2 c. green pepper, diced
1/2 c. onion, diced
1/2 c. tomato, diced
8 to 10 slices bacon, crisply cooked and crumbled, or 1 c. cooked ham, diced
dried oregano to taste

Spread toast cubes in a greased 13"x9" baking pan. Whisk together eggs and milk; pour over toast. Sprinkle with one cup of cheese. Bake, uncovered, at 350 degrees for 30 to 35 minutes. Top with remaining cheese and other ingredients; bake an additional 25 minutes. Makes 6 to 8 servings.

Bacon Skillet Breakfast

Betsy Compton
Fort Gibson, OK

This dish is mmm-mmm good...so good, we enjoy it for dinner too!

8 slices bacon
4 potatoes, peeled and diced
1/2 c. onion, diced
4 eggs, beaten
1 c. shredded Cheddar cheese

In a skillet over medium heat, cook bacon until crisp. Remove bacon from skillet to a paper towel; add potatoes and onion to drippings in skillet. Cook potatoes and onion until tender; drain well but do not remove from skillet. In a separate non-stick skillet over low heat, scramble eggs until set but still moist. Spoon eggs over potatoes; layer with bacon and cheese. Cover and cook over low heat until cheese is melted. Serves 2 to 4.

Dorothy's Sticky Buns

Mary Beth LaPorte
Escanaba, MI

Twenty years ago, when I began teaching at a small country school, we had a foster grandmother who would bake these buns in the morning for our school staff. They always disappeared immediately! I bake them often for family & friends, especially during the holidays. Serve them with an egg bake and fresh fruit. What a treat!

24 frozen dinner rolls
3-oz. pkg. cook & serve
   butterscotch pudding
1/2 c. sugar
1/4 c. brown sugar, packed

1 t. cinnamon
1 c. pecan halves, or more to
   taste
1/2 c. butter, melted

Arrange frozen dinner rolls in a greased 13"x9" baking pan, making rows of 4 rolls by 6 rolls. In a small bowl, stir together dry pudding mix, sugars and cinnamon. Sprinkle mixture evenly over rolls; sprinkle pecans on top. Drizzle melted butter evenly over rolls. Tent rolls with aluminum foil; seal around the edges. Place pan in a cold oven and allow to rise for 8 hours to overnight. Remove pan from oven; preheat oven to 350 degrees. Remove foil and bake for 30 minutes, or until golden. To serve, let stand for a few minutes, then run a knife around the edge of the pan to loosen. Invert pan onto a baking sheet. Makes 2 dozen.

We all love breakfast foods, but it seems like there's never time to linger over them in the morning. Enjoy an unhurried breakfast with your family...at dinnertime! A simple omelet or frittata is perfect. Just add a basket of muffins, fresh fruit and a steamy pot of tea. Relax and enjoy!

Stir-Crazy Cake

Linda Murray
Brentwood, NH

I've been making this cake for 30 years...my family never tires of its moist, deep chocolate flavor and crisp cinnamon top. The recipe is quick to fix because you mix it right in the pan. No greasing or flouring needed and no messy mixing bowl to wash!

2-1/2 c. all-purpose flour
1-3/4 c. sugar, divided
1/2 c. baking cocoa
2 t. baking soda
1/2 t. salt

2/3 c. oil
2 T. vinegar
1 T. vanilla extract
2 c. cold brewed coffee or water
1/2 t. cinnamon

Add flour, 1-1/2 cups sugar, cocoa, baking soda and salt to an ungreased 13"x9" metal baking pan. Stir with a fork to mix; use a spoon to form 3 wells in flour mixture. Pour oil into one well, vinegar into one well and vanilla into one well. Pour cold coffee or water over all ingredients; stir quickly with fork until well mixed. Do not beat. Combine cinnamon and remaining sugar; sprinkle evenly over batter. Bake at 350 degrees for 35 to 40 minutes, until cake tests done with a toothpick. Makes 12 servings.

Make a game of table talk! Write fun questions on slips of paper... what kind of animal would you like to be, what's your favorite time of year, and so on. Pull a different question each night to talk about.

Just-for-Fun Fruit Pizza

Candy-Love Staub
Red Lion, PA

I learned this fun dessert recipe in my 7th grade home economics class. It's a favorite of mine to take to family outings in the summer...always a big hit! Kids love to help make fruit pizza too. We've tried berries of all kinds, as well as sliced kiwi and peaches. You can't go wrong!

8-oz. tube refrigerated crescent
    rolls
1 T. butter, melted
1/2 t. almond extract
4 t. sugar
1-1/2 c. milk

3.4-oz. pkg. instant vanilla
    pudding mix
1 c. frozen whipped topping,
    thawed
3 c. fresh fruit and berries, sliced

Unroll rolls without separating. Press rolls into an ungreased 12" round pizza pan or 13"x9" baking pan; press seams together. In a small bowl, combine butter and almond extract; brush over rolls. Sprinkle with sugar. Bake at 375 degrees for 11 to 13 minutes, until golden. Cool baked crust completely in pan on a wire rack. In a bowl, with an electric mixer on low speed, beat milk and dry pudding mix for one minute. Cover bowl and refrigerate for 10 minutes; fold in whipped topping. Spread pudding mixture evenly over crust. Arrange fruit over pudding. Cover and refrigerate for one to 3 hours; cut into wedges or squares. Makes 8 servings.

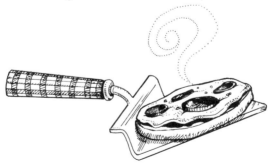

Do you have lots of kids coming over for an after-game party? Make it easy with do-it-yourself tacos or mini pizzas...guests can add their own favorite toppings. Round out the menu with pitchers of soft drinks and a yummy dessert pizza. Simple and fun!

Homemade Chocolate Syrup

Karen Sullivan
Louisville, KY

My mother used to make this scrumptious ice cream topping for me as a treat when I was little. Now that I'm an adult, it's still my #1 comfort food...wonderful drizzled over brownies too.

1 c. sugar	1/4 c. milk
3 T. baking cocoa	1 t. creamy peanut butter

Combine sugar and cocoa in a small saucepan. Add milk and bring to a boil over medium-high heat; boil for one minute. Place peanut butter in a heat-proof bowl; pour hot mixture over peanut butter. Stir to blend. Serve warm. Makes 2 to 4 servings.

Best Caramel Sauce

Sheila Murray
Tehachapi, CA

I used to make this yummy sauce to serve with apple slices at school parties. Of course, it's wonderful over ice cream too!

14-oz. pkg. caramels, unwrapped	1/3 c. milk
1/4 c. butter, sliced	1/2 t. cinnamon

Combine all ingredients in a microwave-safe bowl. Microwave on high setting for 2 to 3 minutes, stirring after each minute, until caramels are melted. Serve warm. Makes 4 to 6 servings.

Instant ice cream social! Alongside pints of ice cream, set out toppings like sliced bananas, peanuts, maraschino cherries, hot fudge and whipped cream. Don't forget the jimmies!

INDEX

INDEX

INDEX

U.S. to Metric Recipe Equivalents

Volume Measurements

1/4 teaspoon	1 mL
1/2 teaspoon	2 mL
1 teaspoon	5 mL
1 tablespoon = 3 teaspoons	15 mL
2 tablespoons = 1 fluid ounce	30 mL
1/4 cup	60 mL
1/3 cup	75 mL
1/2 cup = 4 fluid ounces	125 mL
1 cup = 8 fluid ounces	250 mL
2 cups = 1 pint =16 fluid ounces	500 mL
4 cups = 1 quart	1 L

Weights

1 ounce	30 g
4 ounces	120 g
8 ounces	225 g
16 ounces = 1 pound	450 g

Oven Temperatures

300° F	150° C
325° F	160° C
350° F	180° C
375° F	190° C
400° F	200° C
450° F	230° C

Baking Pan Sizes

Square

8x8x2 inches	2 L = 20x20x5 cm
9x9x2 inches	2.5 L = 23x23x5 cm

Rectangular

13x9x2 inches	3.5 L = 33x23x5 cm

Loaf

9x5x3 inches	2 L = 23x13x7 cm

Round

8x1-1/2 inches	1.2 L = 20x4 cm
9x1-1/2 inches	1.5 L = 23x4 cm